Upper Room

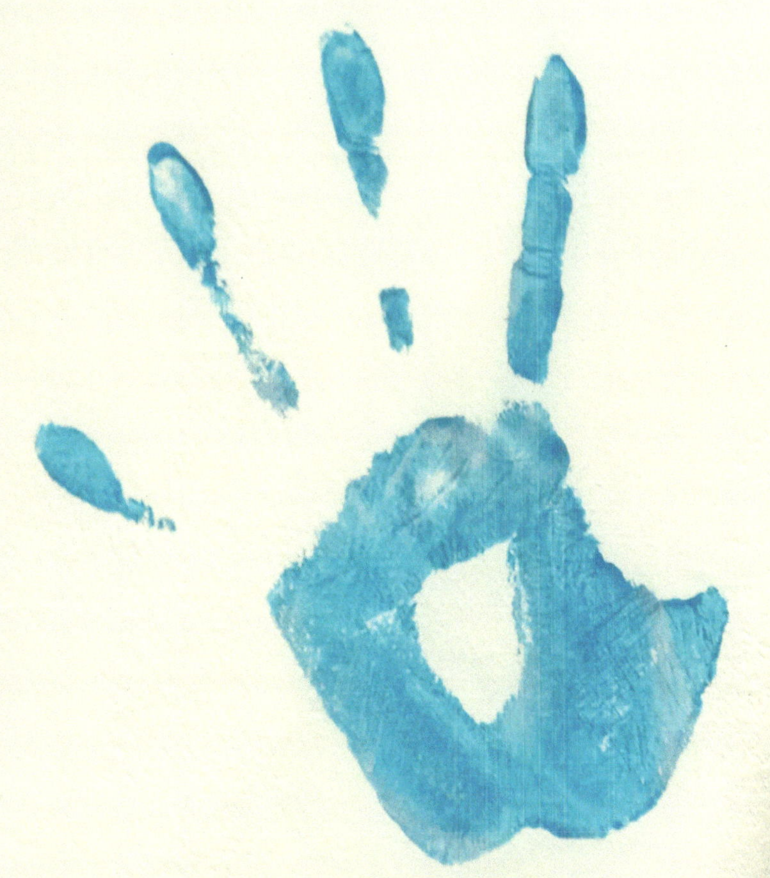

Deborah Last

Published by Deborah Last
First Published in 2014

ISBN 978-0-9928842-9-1

Deborah Last, Walpole House, Stowe School, Buckingham, MK18 5DF

www.deborahlast.co.uk

Book designed by Ollie Goddard (www.olliegoddard.co.uk)
Photography by Roger Goddard (www.rogergoddard.co.uk), Andy Winter

Dedication: to my mother and my daughters; may you always feel amazing about who you are as you are - fearfully and wonderfully made; and to all women everywhere who doubt their beauty.

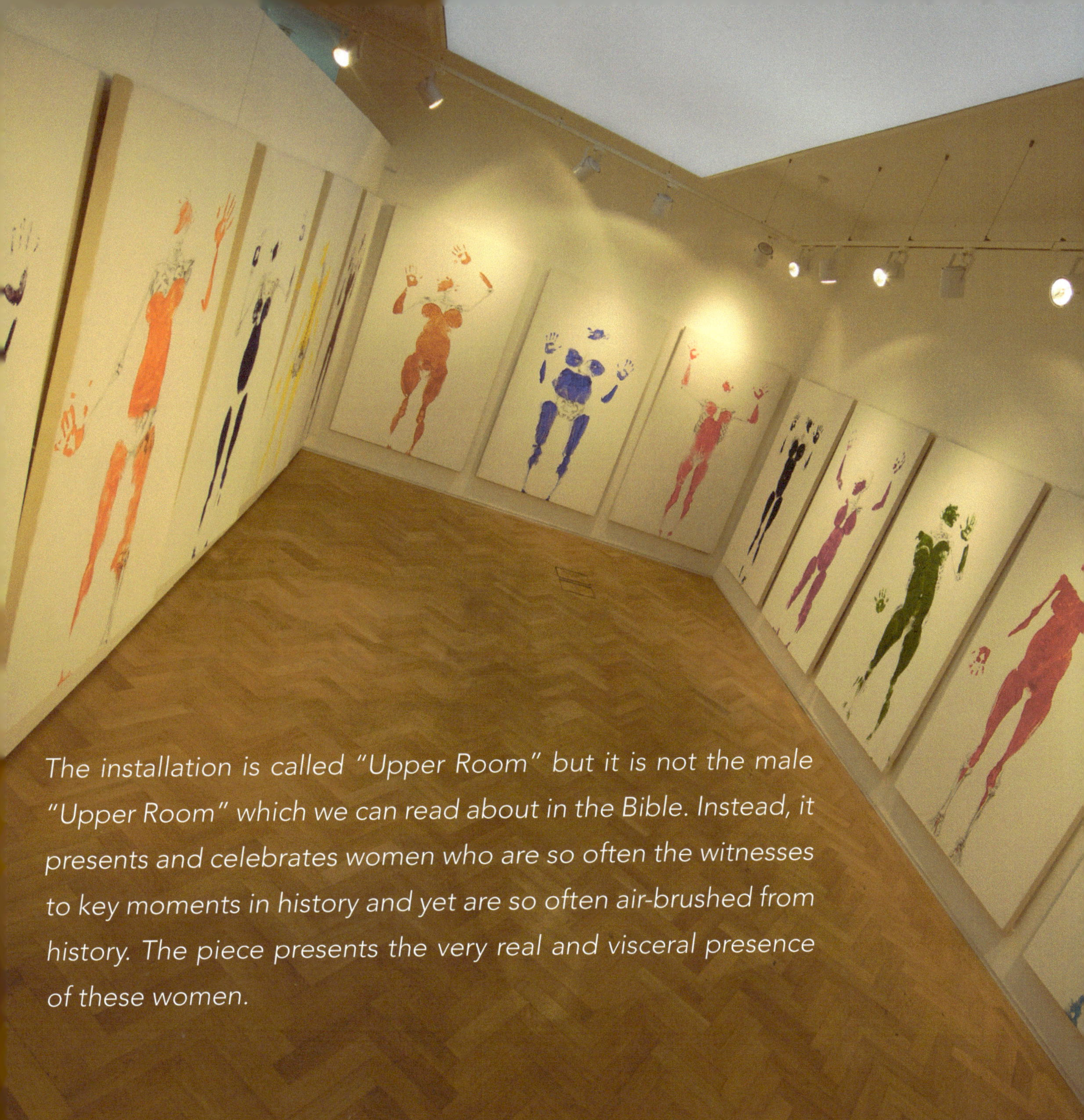

The installation is called "Upper Room" but it is not the male "Upper Room" which we can read about in the Bible. Instead, it presents and celebrates women who are so often the witnesses to key moments in history and yet are so often air-brushed from history. The piece presents the very real and visceral presence of these women.

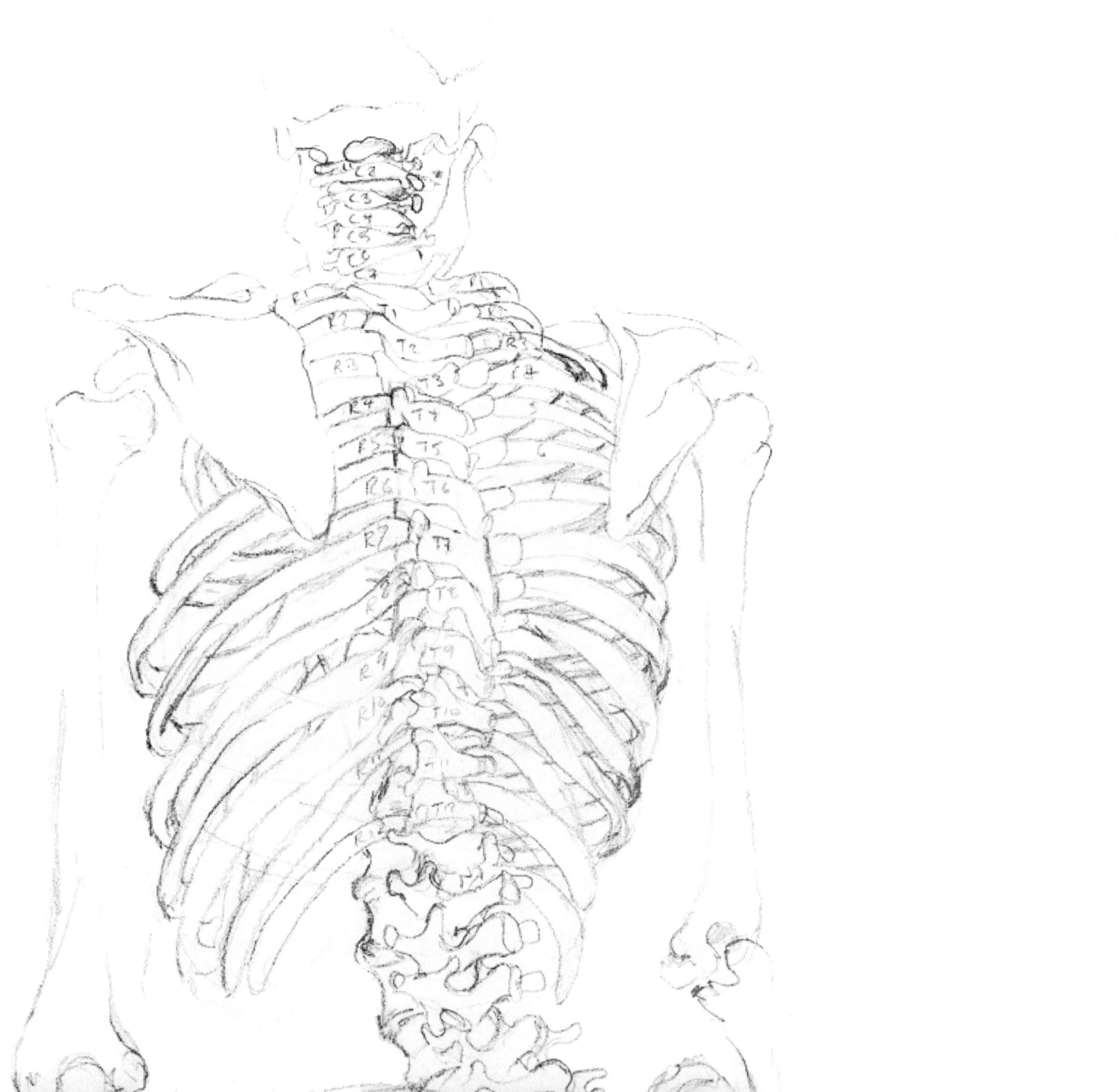
C2
C3
C4
C5
C6
C7
R1
T1
R2
T2
R3
T3
R4
T4
R5
T5
R6
T6
R7
T7
T8
R9
T9
R10
T10
T11
T12

Song of Songs 4

New International Version (NIV)

He

4 How beautiful you are, my darling!
Oh, how beautiful!
Your eyes behind your veil are doves.
Your hair is like a flock of goats
descending from the hills of Gilead.
2 Your teeth are like a flock of sheep just shorn,
coming up from the washing.
Each has its twin;
not one of them is alone.
3 Your lips are like a scarlet ribbon;
your mouth is lovely.
Your temples behind your veil
are like the halves of a pomegranate.
4 Your neck is like the tower of David,
built with courses of stone[a];
on it hang a thousand shields,
all of them shields of warriors.
5 Your breasts are like two fawns,
like twin fawns of a gazelle
that browse among the lilies.
6 Until the day breaks
and the shadows flee,
I will go to the mountain of myrrh
and to the hill of incense.
7 You are altogether beautiful, my darling;
there is no flaw in you.
8 Come with me from Lebanon, my bride,
come with me from Lebanon.
Descend from the crest of Amana,
from the top of Senir, the summit of Hermon,
from the lions' dens
and the mountain haunts of leopards.
9 You have stolen my heart, my sister, my bride;
you have stolen my heart
with one glance of your eyes,
with one jewel of your necklace.
10 How delightful is your love, my sister, my bride!
How much more pleasing is your love than wine,
and the fragrance of your perfume
more than any spice!
11 Your lips drop sweetness as the honeycomb, my bride;
milk and honey are under your tongue.
The fragrance of your garments
is like the fragrance of Lebanon.
12 You are a garden locked up, my sister, my bride;
you are a spring enclosed, a sealed fountain.
13 Your plants are an orchard of pomegranates
with choice fruits,
with henna and nard,
14 nard and saffron,
calamus and cinnamon,
with every kind of incense tree,
with myrrh and aloes
and all the finest spices.
15 You are a garden fountain,
a well of flowing water
streaming down from Lebanon.

The Story Starts...

"Upper Room" is the culmination of more than three years work. My artwork has held a narrative standpoint from the outset. As a small child, I clearly remember waking early in my room, sitting on the floor with my pens and drawing a house or a garden. As I drew, I would create in my head the story of the people who lived there. Story-telling and painting have gone hand in hand with my work ever since. I've told the stories of women and motherhood; ancient stories that sing through the ages, stories of faith and life.

"Upper Room" is the coming together of many years of thought and dialogue about body image and self-worth. I spent 16 years working as an art teacher and most of those working within a school boarding house, both here in the UK and in India. Those years taught me much about young women and their concepts of themselves, alongside their perception of beauty within the context of peer groups and culture; what beauty might be and what striving after it might do to self-worth. This piece takes that dialogue to a wider audience as part of an ongoing investigation and journey.

Of course it has been enormously informative raising my two beautiful daughters. Knowing that their self-esteem is a precious and wonderful thing, I have watched it blossom and grow along a bumpy and challenging road as they have grown into young women. Having also raised a son, it must be noted here, that the road for boys is equally challenging in a world that places demands and expectations on them to be modern men, gentle and masculine, sensitive and fit, understanding and able to sport a perfect six-pack! But that perhaps is another piece of work...

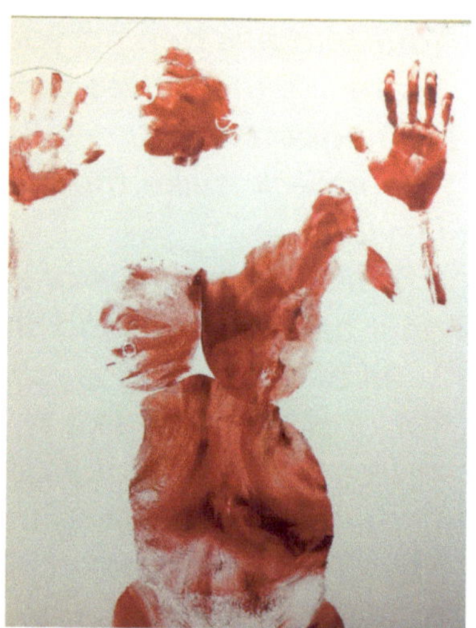

This is the first body print

Body Prints...

In May 2012 whilst attending a wedding, I was asked if I would produce a body print for a friend's friend who was pregnant, as a record of the pregnancy. I had already started a series of work that I was calling "The Beauty Series". I wanted to start a dialogue about what we perceive to be beautiful. So often a beautiful person has something deeper. I had begun a painting of my mum laughing and had recorded her talking about what beauty is and her memories involving beauty.

The sound I had recorded was fantastic and moving but somehow the portrait painting felt wrong. Doing the body print of the pregnant woman was an extraordinary moment. I finally felt that the concept matched my desire to work within the contemporary context and still tell the story visually.

In the same way that Anthony Gormley uses his own body to cast the figures for his work, I was interested in using the body as a primary tool. There is an element of replication of self in the work that is truly of the person printing produced with their body; an imprint of their own uniqueness and beauty – giving something of oneself, a lasting moment of time. I had to work out how I would do the body print to ensure that it wasn't a big smudge across the canvas. Initially, I primed large pieces of un-stretched canvas and printed on to these. The very first prints were tried out on A1 sheets of paper.

As soon as I had prints I started to play with them. My first concept was to add background colour almost descriptive of water or the womb.

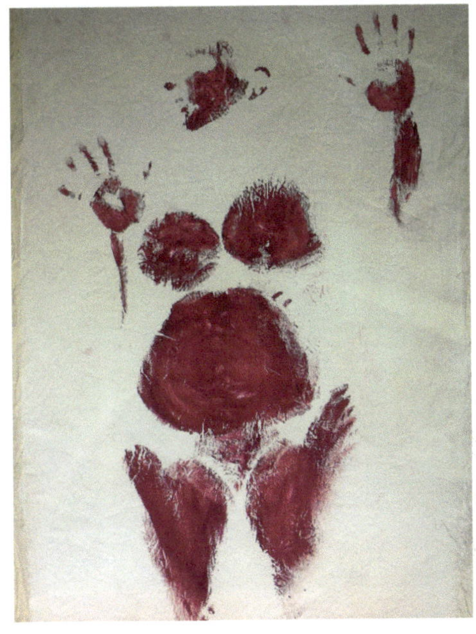

The pregnant woman

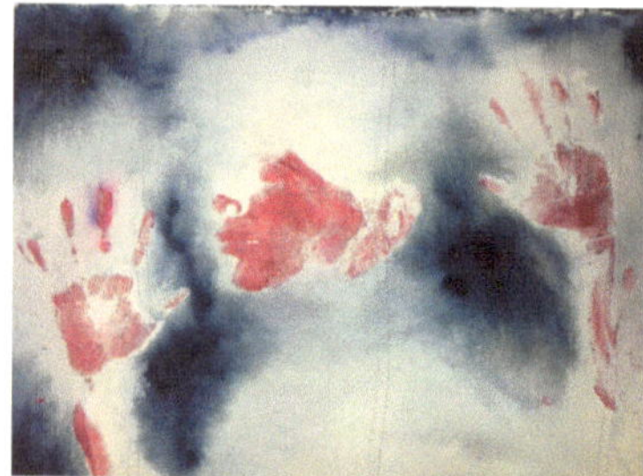

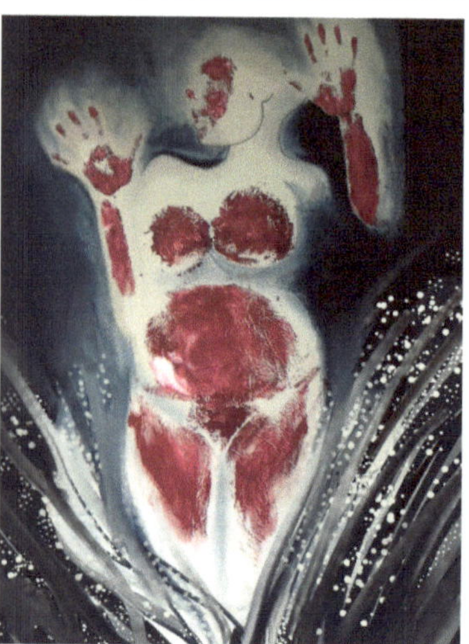

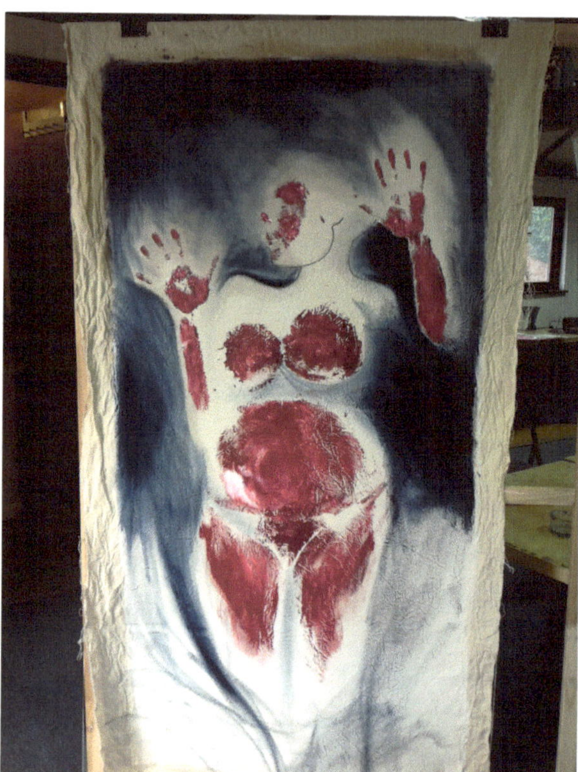

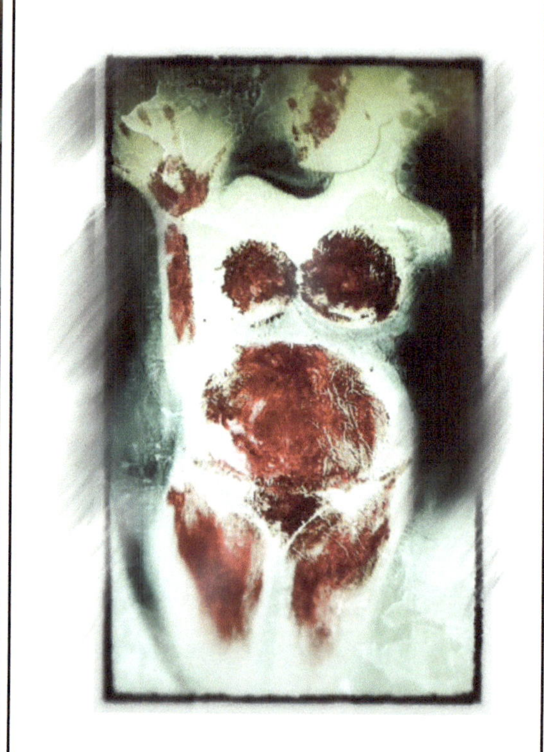

Working with the iPad as a drawing tool, I manipulated the body print in various programs, but it soon became clear that the images were becoming too complicated and cluttered. They were losing their sophistication.

Adding the Sound...

I now had questions to answer; how to display the work? How to include the sound and what format should the painting take? I had been very excited by the exhibition at the Tate of the work of Susan Hiller and in particular the piece Witness (2000) this very soon became the inspiration for the sound. I wanted the sound to be as if you were overhearing a group of women talking but as you draw close an individual voice can be heard.

I feel so strongly that women can be trapped by the ideas of beauty and what is and is not acceptable. It is a brilliant thing to accept who you are and to celebrate that, but so often we are derailed by the images we see through the media and the unreality of social media. I wanted to present women at a major event in history, one that tapped into a key moment of faith too; a chance to challenge the norms. I was reminded of the Chris Offli piece "The Upper Room" and the logistics of this piece. I had worked out a way to body print that meant I could leave the canvas on the 6 by 4 foot stretcher bars. And these leant themselves to display not unlike Ofili's The Upper Room. Perfect, a brilliant event and layout for the work.

I bought fifteen 46 x 72 inch canvas frames and my art assistant, James, and I set to work stretching the canvas onto them. I got a local company to make a board to fit exactly inside the back of the frames so it was possible to body print onto canvas while they were on the stretcher bars. I had to use canvas so that the sound could go behind the prints therefore, the canvases acting like a big speaker case.

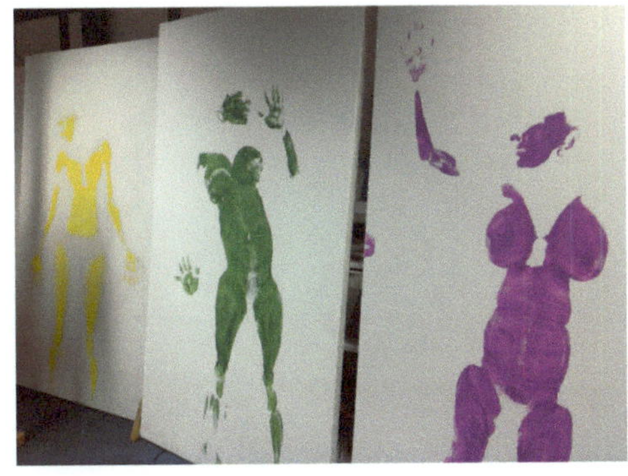

The first three prints. The yellow one was printed off the stretcher bars but by the time I was doing the green and purple one I had worked out a better way of doing them; much easier and quicker.

Adding Anatomical Drawing...

Around this time I went on an anatomy course at the Ruskin School of Art, Oxford. It was hugely inspiring and exciting. As I came back, I knew I had discovered the perfect addition to the installation: anatomical drawings.

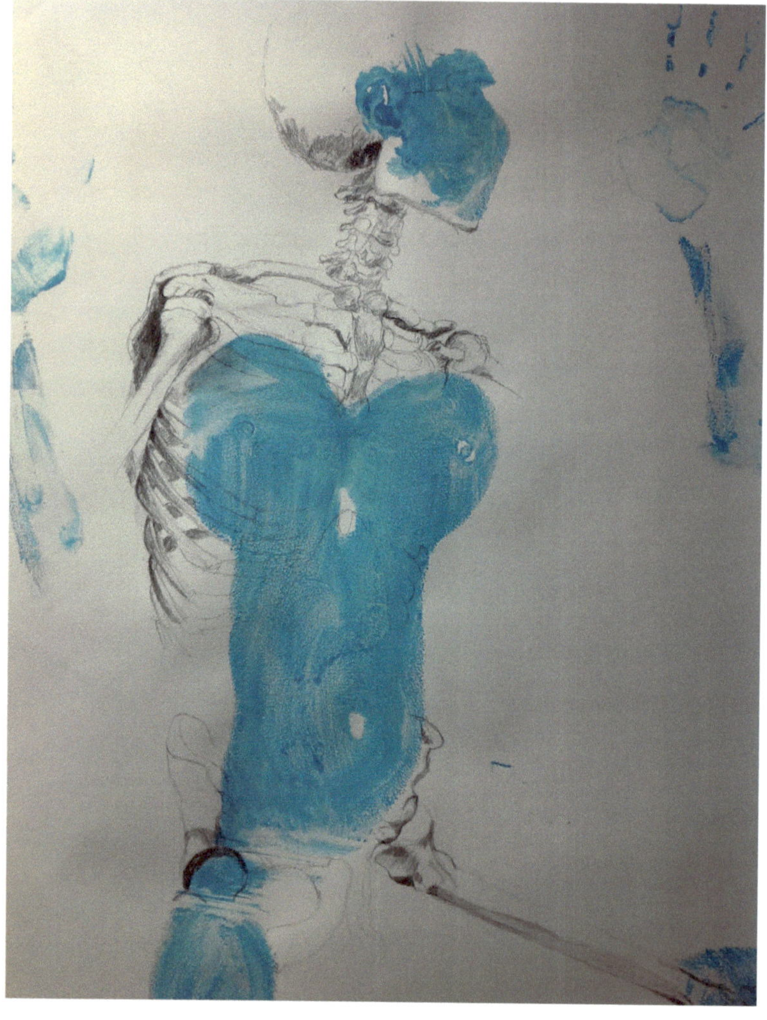

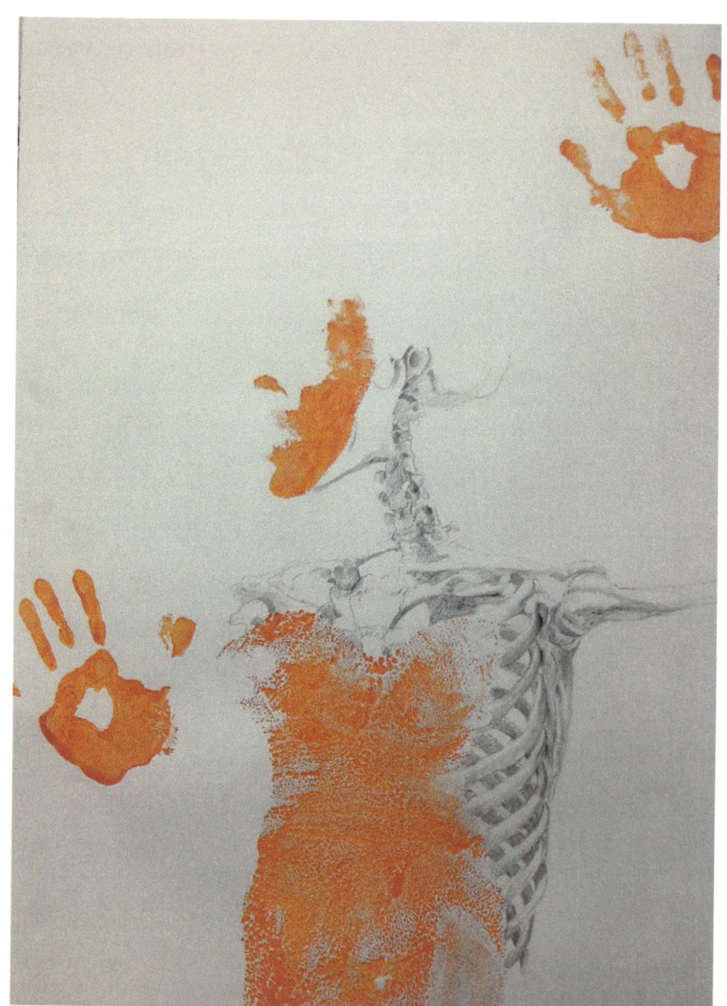

13 For you created my inmost being;
you knit me together in my mother's womb.
14 I praise you because I am fearfully and wonderfully made;
your works are wonderful,
I know that full well. Psalm 139

The Conversation

By February 2013 the concept was fully formed, I had enlisted the help of Daniel Hobden, a sound designer and was busily recruiting for and printing the body prints. I wanted lots of different women to do the sound as well which meant those who did not want to print could take part in the sound.

I asked the following questions:

What do you think beauty is?

Why do women spend so much time trying to make themselves look beautiful?

Can you remember being called pretty or beautiful as a child?

Can you recall a moment when you felt beautiful?

How do you think your beliefs affect your body image and self-worth?

Doing the sound was amazing; hearing what each woman had to say about beauty and their experiences. So many of the women talked about beauty being more than external...

"I think beauty is a state of mind perhaps as much a physical attribute. It's the way that you behave; you can act beautifully.... or you can behave disgustingly so I think it's a dualism between the two. We focus on the external attributes of beauty but it's as much from within as external."

Canvas 1

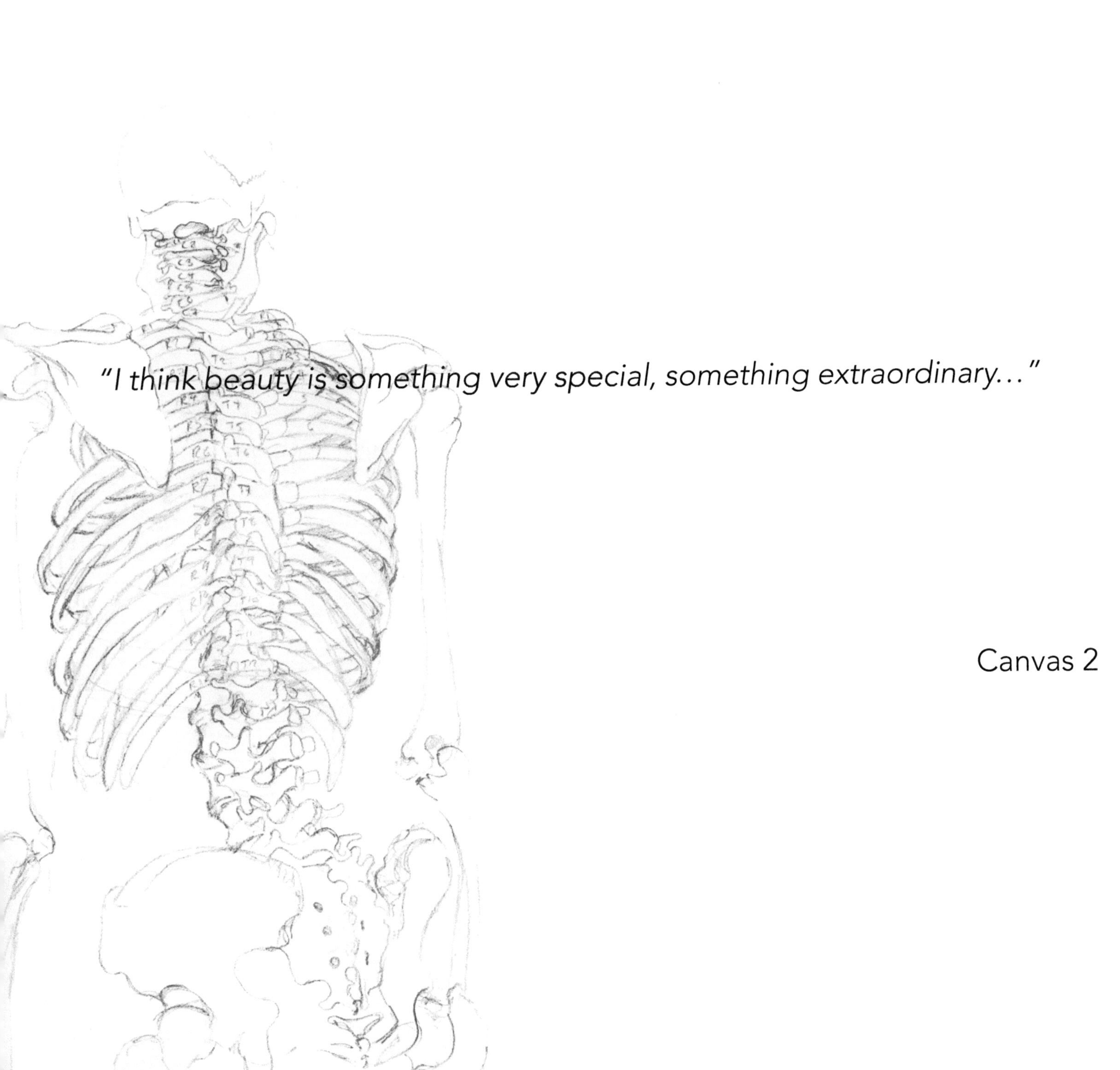

"I think beauty is something very special, something extraordinary…"

Canvas 2

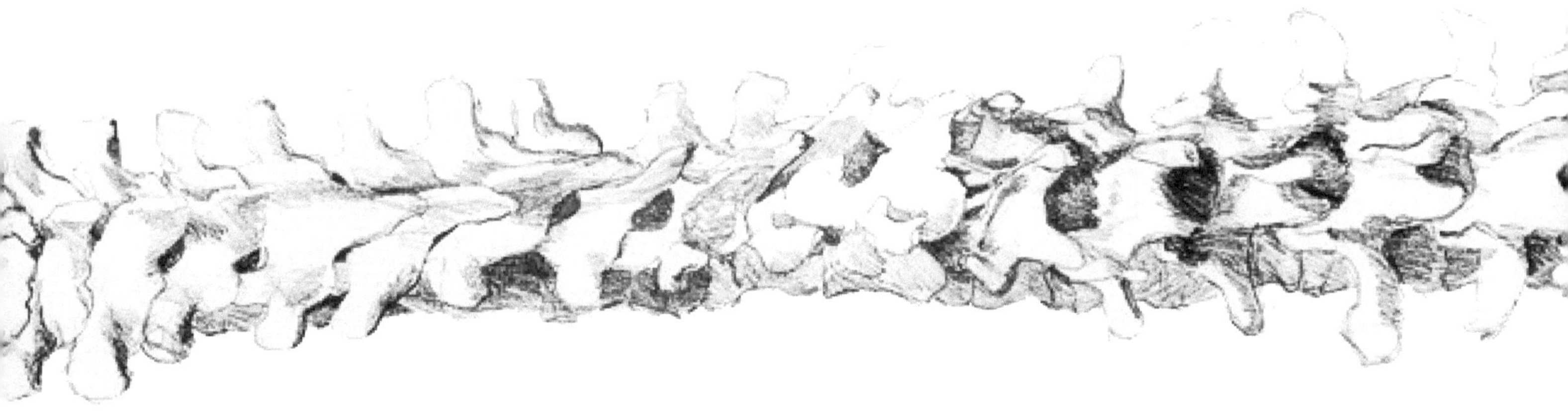

"I think beauty is fabulous actually, so when I see somebody that looks in my mind beautiful they are happy with it; they look comfortable, they look glowing, they look just natural as well…."

Canvas 5

(All the sound from the canvases can be heard by using the QR codes at the back of the book.)

"Upper Room" crosses boundaries, having a message in different contexts; in a school, a place of worship, an art gallery or public space. It is important to ask how do our beliefs about ourselves, our culture, our faith, if we have one, affect our body image and self-image. The body prints give few clues to the age, culture or colour of the woman who printed. This anonymity adds universality to the concept which extends the value of the discussion across boundaries to all women, indeed to men and women alike, it is important to ask how we view women: how do we as societies across the globe engender a good body image in women from youth to old age?

Asking the question "Do you remember being called beautiful or pretty as a child?" threw up so many reactions from the straight "No" to wonderful descriptions of childhood memories.

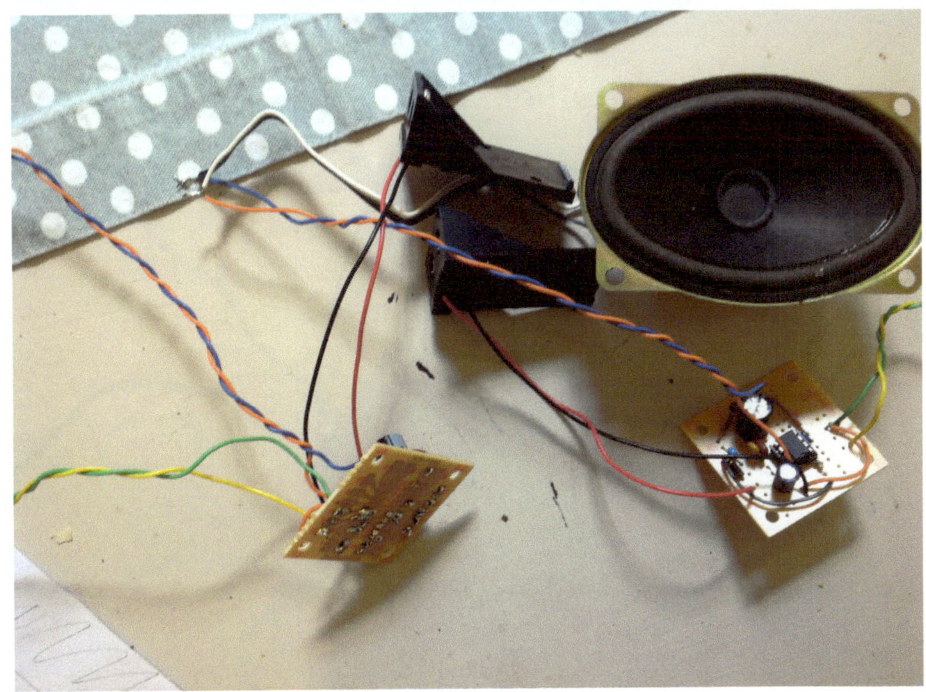

The speaker and circuit

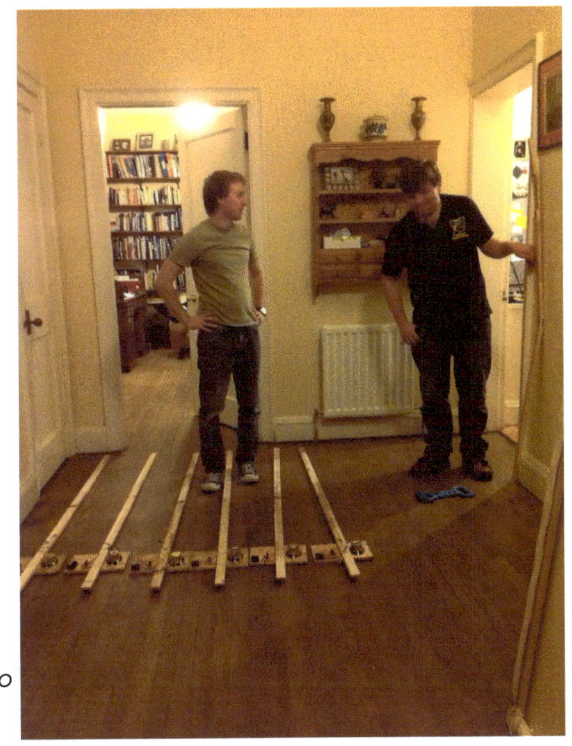

Daniel and Luke beginning to put the speakers together.

Drawing It All Together...

By the summer of 2013, all the prints had been done and I was busy drawing onto the canvases and using up lots of pencils...

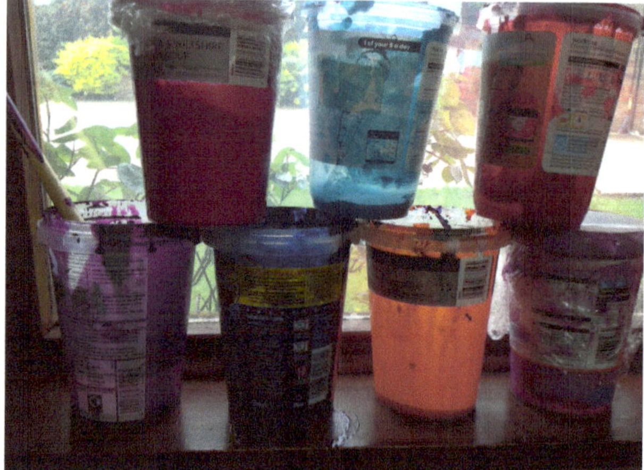

The paint pots from some of the prints

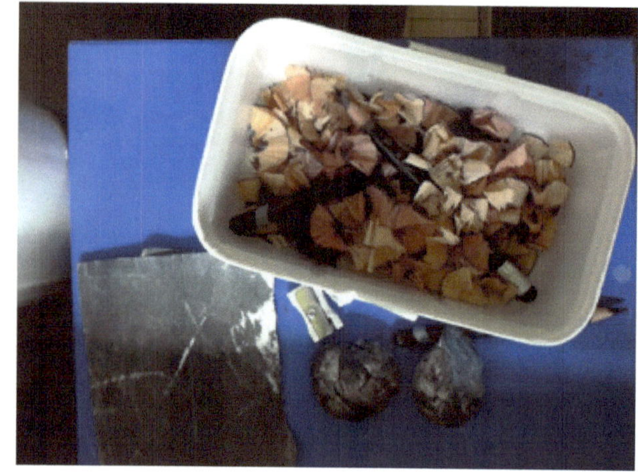

Using up a lot of pencils!

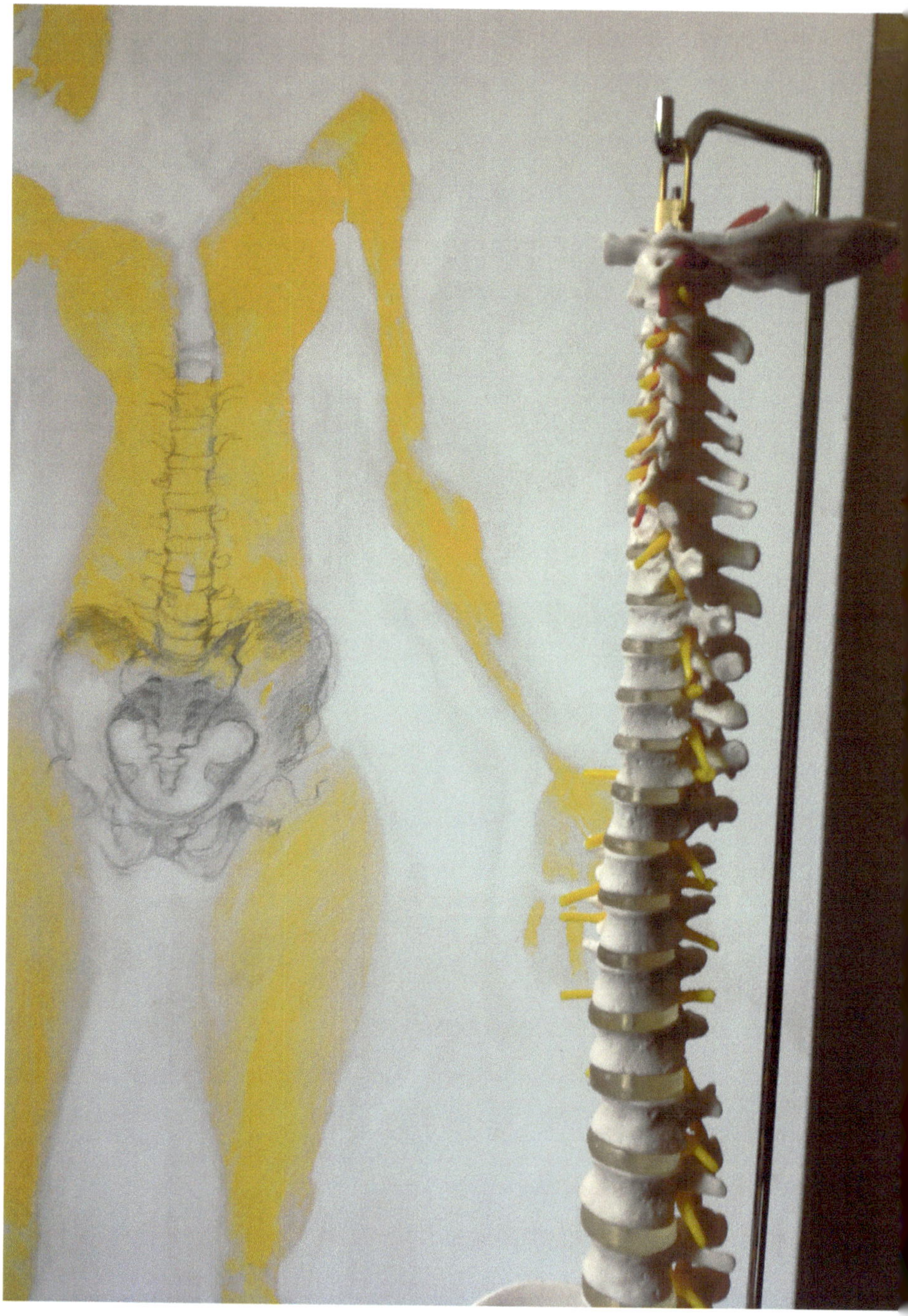

Drawing the spine and pelvis for the yellow canvas

The 13th canvas is in the position of Christ and I wanted Christ to be in the womb. I needed to work out how this would look as a foetal skeleton, without it looking macabre. I could not have the foetal skull facing out fully as this looked too creepy.

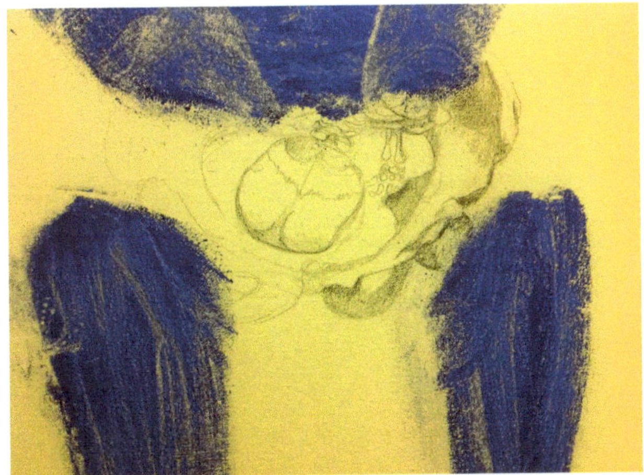

The foetal skeleton, skull drawn facing backwards

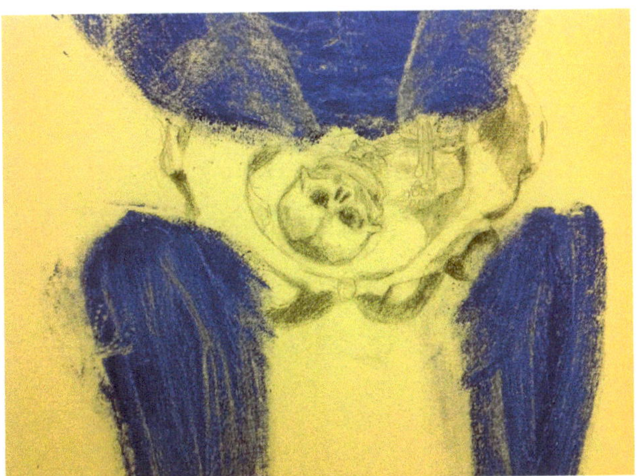

The foetal skeleton, skull drawn facing forwards

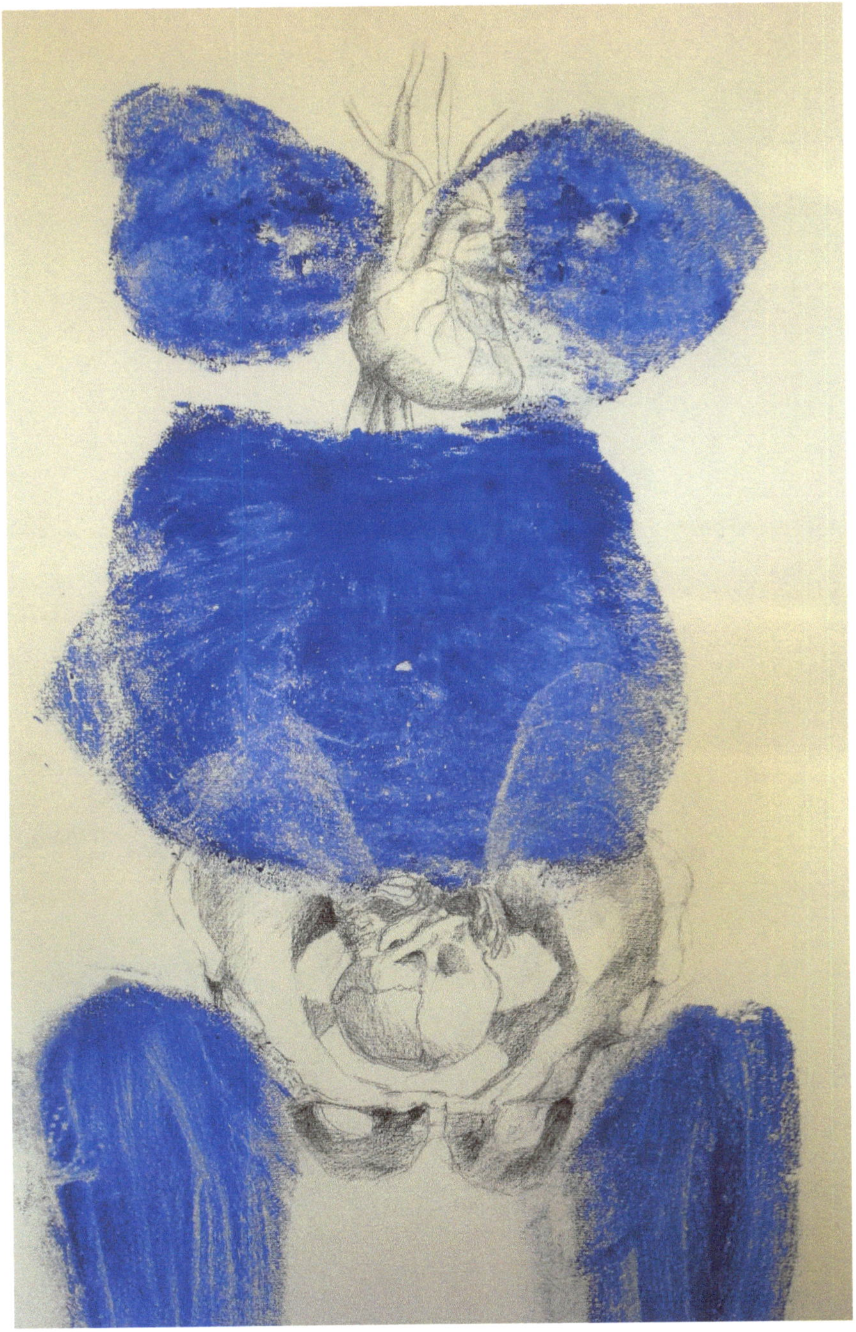

The foetal skull drawn from the side on the 13th Canvas with the addition of the mothers' heart.

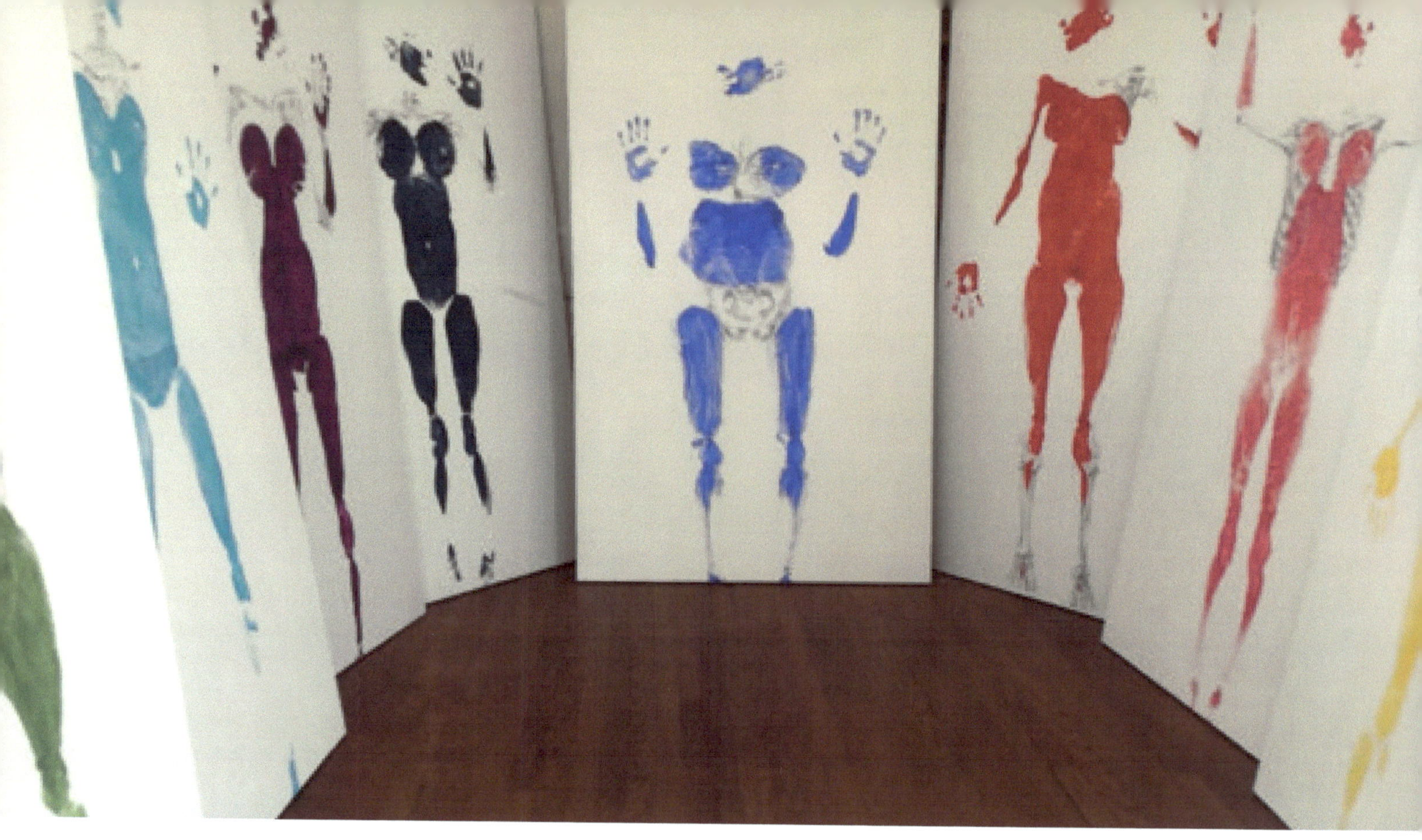

Some of the canvases grouped together tonally. This was not how I would finally choose to arrange them.

At last all the canvases were together and I was able to get them out and begin to view them as they might look as a grouping, albeit at home in a cleared room!

Finally the first exhibition of Upper Room was assembled; a chance to hear and see it fully and to begin to work out all the little tweaks to the sound. Visually it was complete but changes were needed to adjust the sound and make it curator friendly. As I write this the final adjustments are awaiting completion, applications have been sent for funding and the process of putting it together is drawing to a conclusion. It has been seen both at Stowe School in Buckinghamshire and at Lord Wandsworth College, a school in Hampshire and begins its tour around the country. As it goes on its journey I hope to add other voices to the sound and each time it is shown there will be more voices and more thoughts to hear.

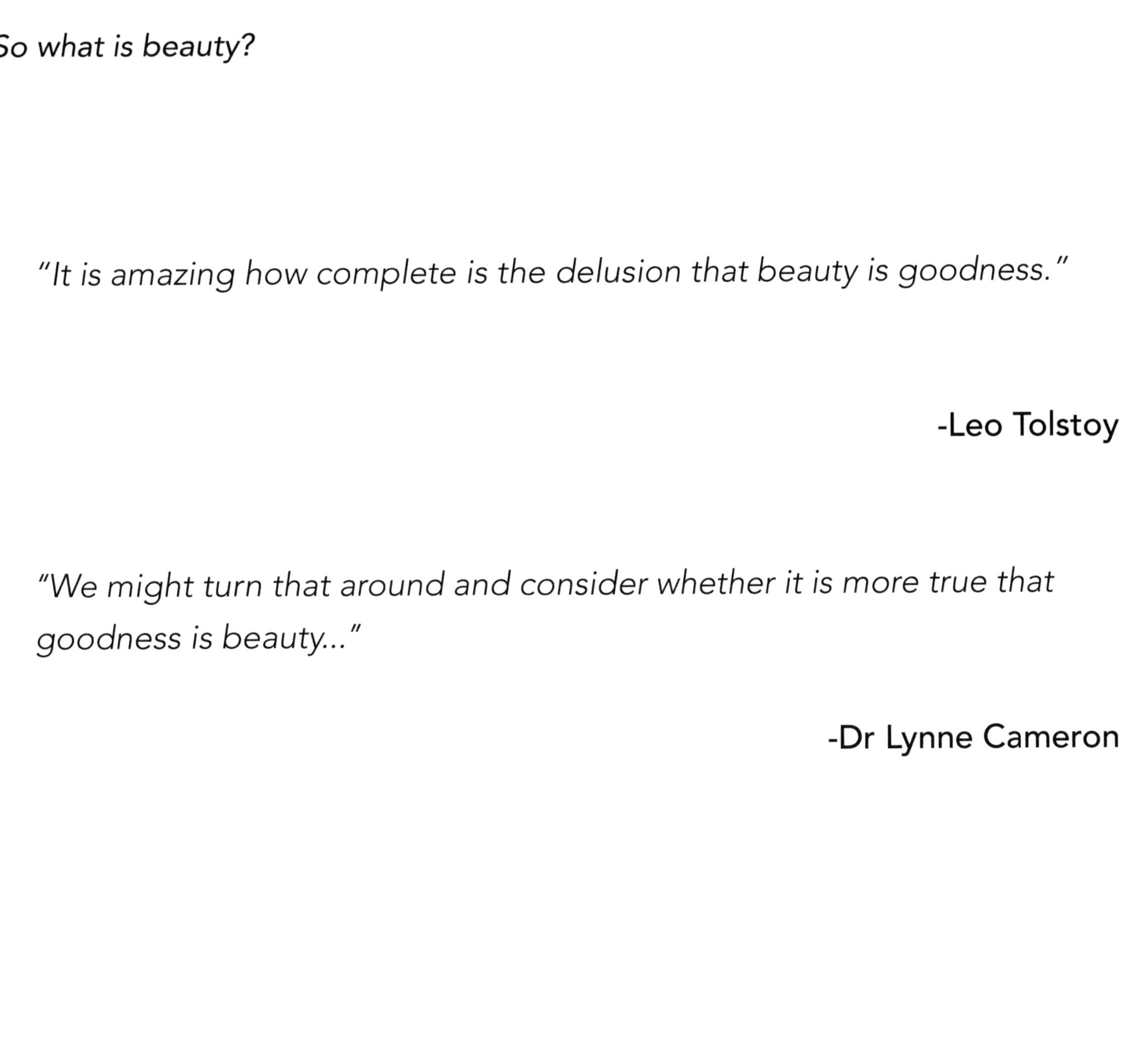

So what is beauty?

"It is amazing how complete is the delusion that beauty is goodness."

-Leo Tolstoy

"We might turn that around and consider whether it is more true that goodness is beauty..."

-Dr Lynne Cameron

Many of the women who did the sound said that they felt the most beautiful on their wedding day or if they had children the day they gave birth. Both days are a time when they were perhaps giving of themselves to others.

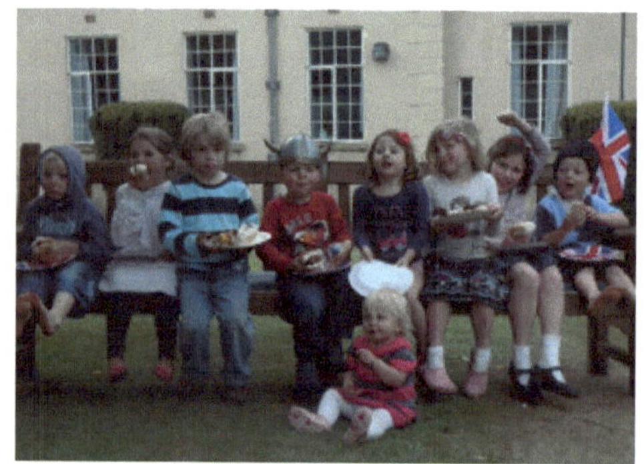

Having children made some feel amazingly beautiful.

I have watched too, many of the wonderful women that I have had the very good fortune to know in my life, both through work, friendship, community and church. Watching them negotiate the different phases of life, through love, birth, death and marriages. I watched too as they succumb to or run from the pressure of the constant presence of social networking, the need to always look good for "selfies"; a photo that might get posted for all to see, the pressure for women to be all things at work and at home.

Perhaps we have lost the time to reflect, to be silent, to see ourselves as we should be seen. Upper Room seeks to stop the viewer and, in the tangled sound of the women's voices, asks them to ask their own questions about themselves, their perceptions and, most deeply, about how their beliefs and world view might affect who they are. The Christian woman believing herself to be a daughter of the living God is going to perhaps have more confidence than one who sees herself only as a rotten sinner.

It might be considered that to take the standpoint that all women are beautiful is naive and simplistic. Clearly, culturally we determine that aesthetically some women are more beautiful than others....and some are. But who they are will vary for each and everyone one of us; and purely aesthetic beauty fades and changes with fashion and time. Everyone's beauty has value – in fact it's priceless – but it's the beauty that shines out from the soul which is more difficult to capture and the world would be duller without it.

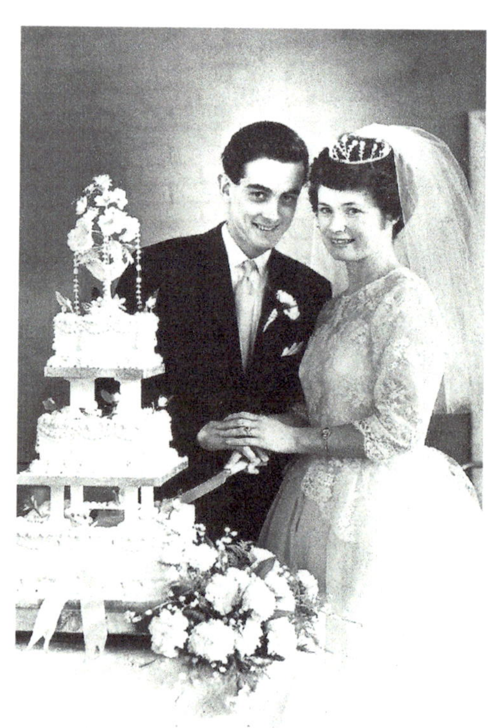

The artist's parents' Wedding Day

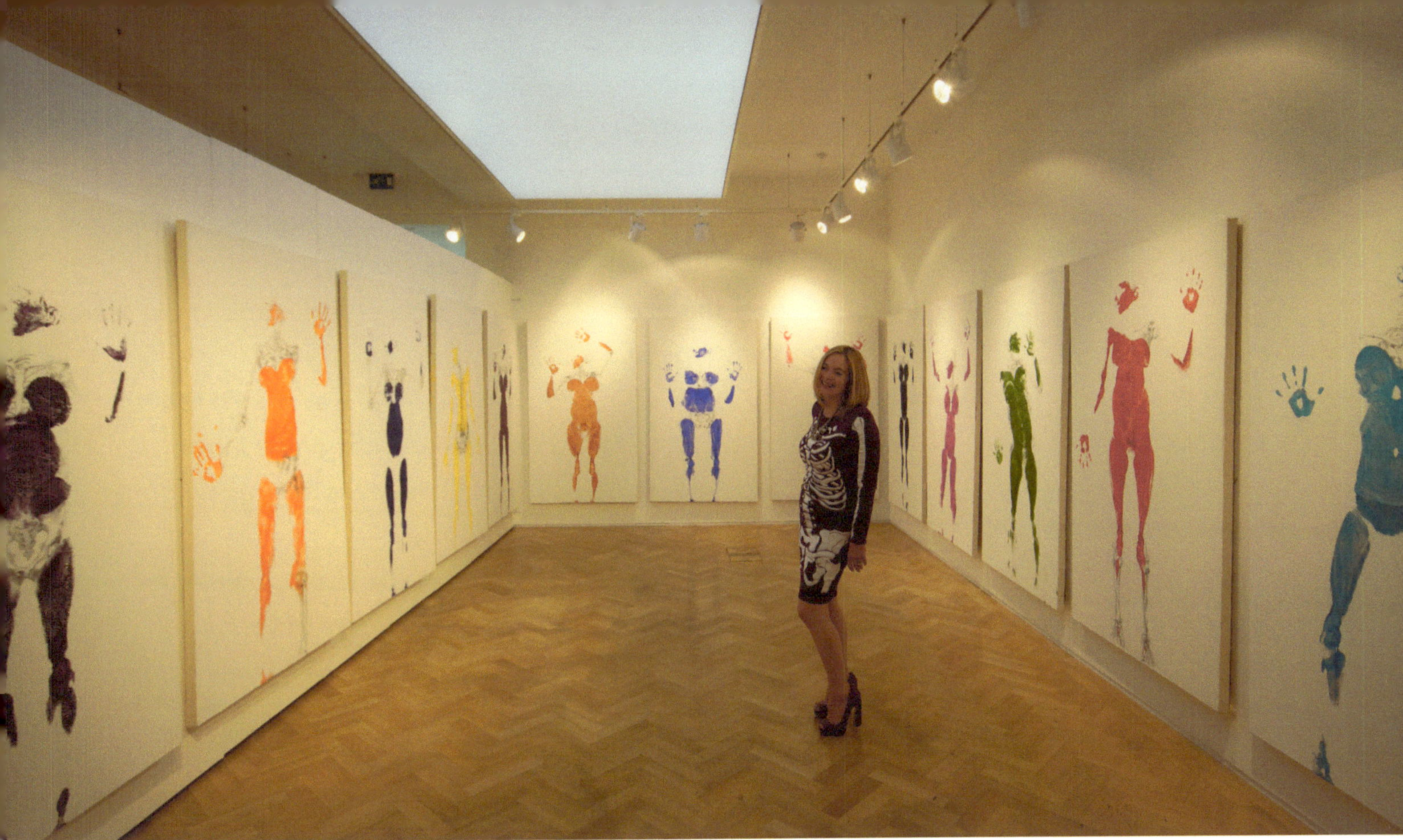

The artist with "Upper Room"at its first showing at Stowe school, Buckingham

It has been an amazing journey producing Upper Room; the affect that it has had on the women involved and the way it has been received as a piece. It was thrilling to see the transformation in the women who left the studio having body printed. They often arrived slightly nervous, wondering what doing it would be like, then having done it left liberated and even elated. I have joked that I could offer this as a therapy. It is clear that it is possible to do something so far out of the norm and in doing it feel amazing; to feel beautiful.

What "Upper Room" proposes is that we are all fearfully and wonderfully made; that we have the potential to "act beautifully" and how ever optimistic it might seem we all have the potential to be the best and most beautiful version of ourselves that we can be.

Psalm 139

New International Version (NIV)

For the director of music. Of David. A psalm.

1 You have searched me, LORD,
and you know me.
2 You know when I sit and when I rise;
you perceive my thoughts from afar.
3 You discern my going out and my lying down;
you are familiar with all my ways.
4 Before a word is on my tongue
you, LORD, know it completely.
5 You hem me in behind and before,
and you lay your hand upon me.
6 Such knowledge is too wonderful for me,
too lofty for me to attain.
7 Where can I go from your Spirit?
Where can I flee from your presence?
8 If I go up to the heavens, you are there;
if I make my bed in the depths, you are there.
9 If I rise on the wings of the dawn,
if I settle on the far side of the sea,
10 even there your hand will guide me,
your right hand will hold me fast.
11 If I say, "Surely the darkness will hide me
and the light become night around me,"
12 even the darkness will not be dark to you;
the night will shine like the day,
for darkness is as light to you.
13 For you created my inmost being;
you knit me together in my mother's womb.
14 I praise you because I am fearfully and wonderfully made;
your works are wonderful,
I know that full well.
15 My frame was not hidden from you
when I was made in the secret place,
when I was woven together in the depths of the earth.
16 Your eyes saw my unformed body;
all the days ordained for me were written in your book
before one of them came to be.
17 How precious to me are your thoughts, God!
How vast is the sum of them!
18 Were I to count them,
they would outnumber the grains of sand—
when I awake, I am still with you.

"Today you are you, that is truer than true. There's no one alive who is youer than you"

-Dr Seuss

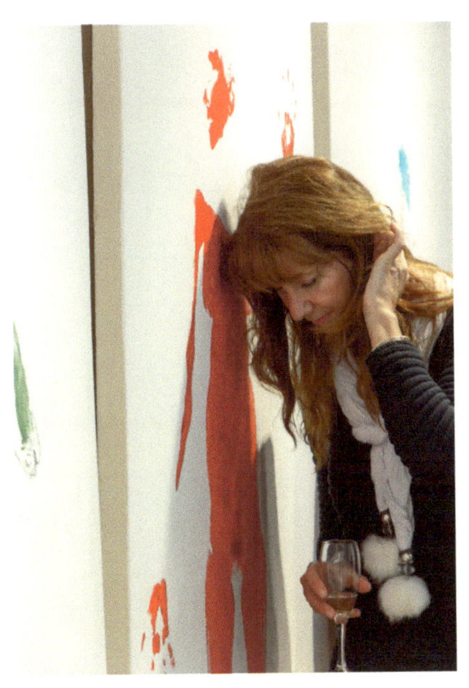

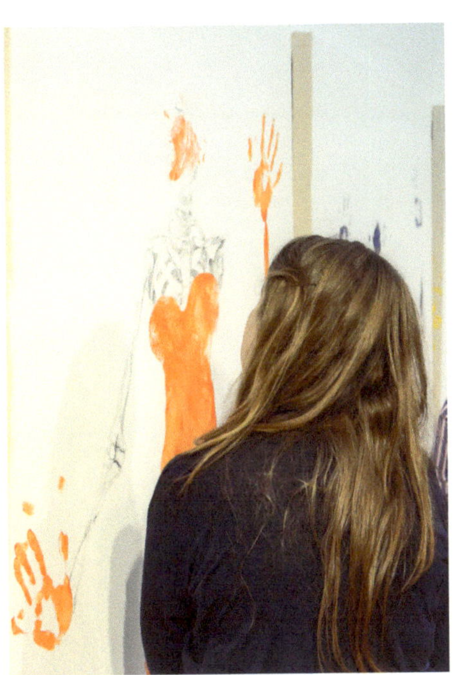

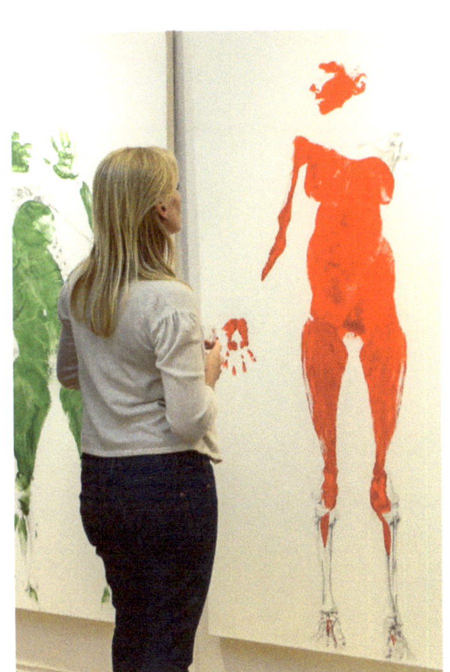

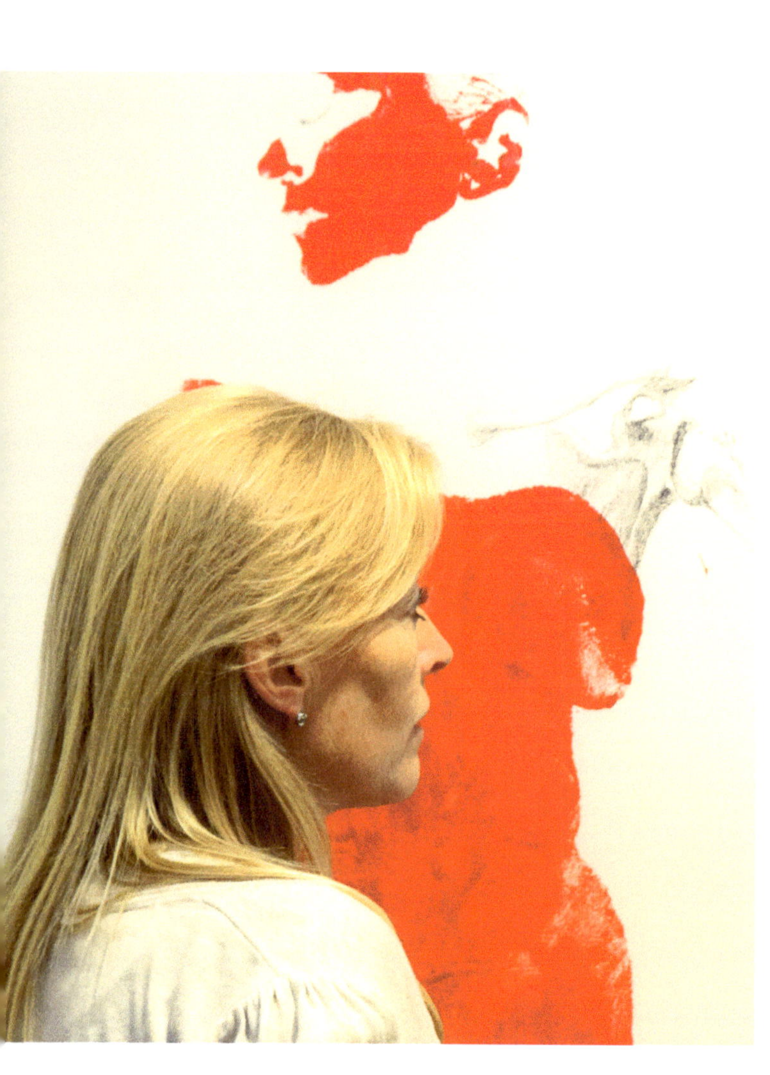

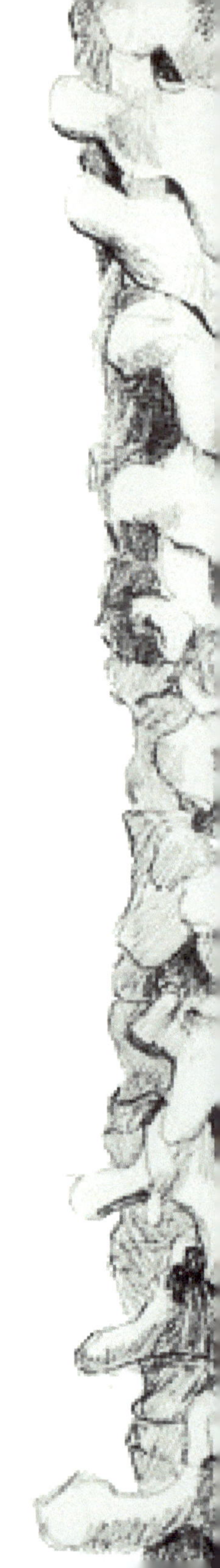

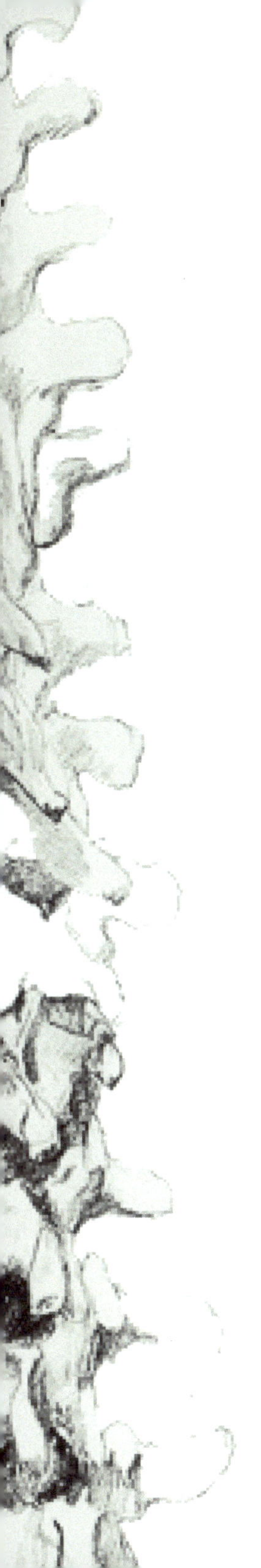

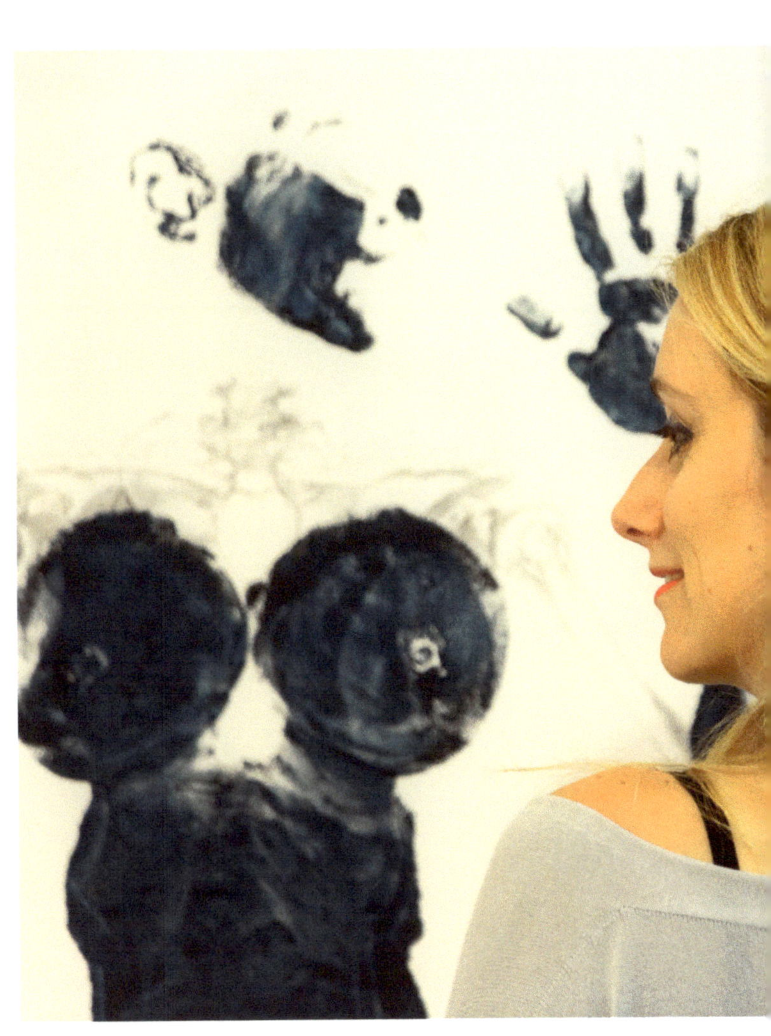

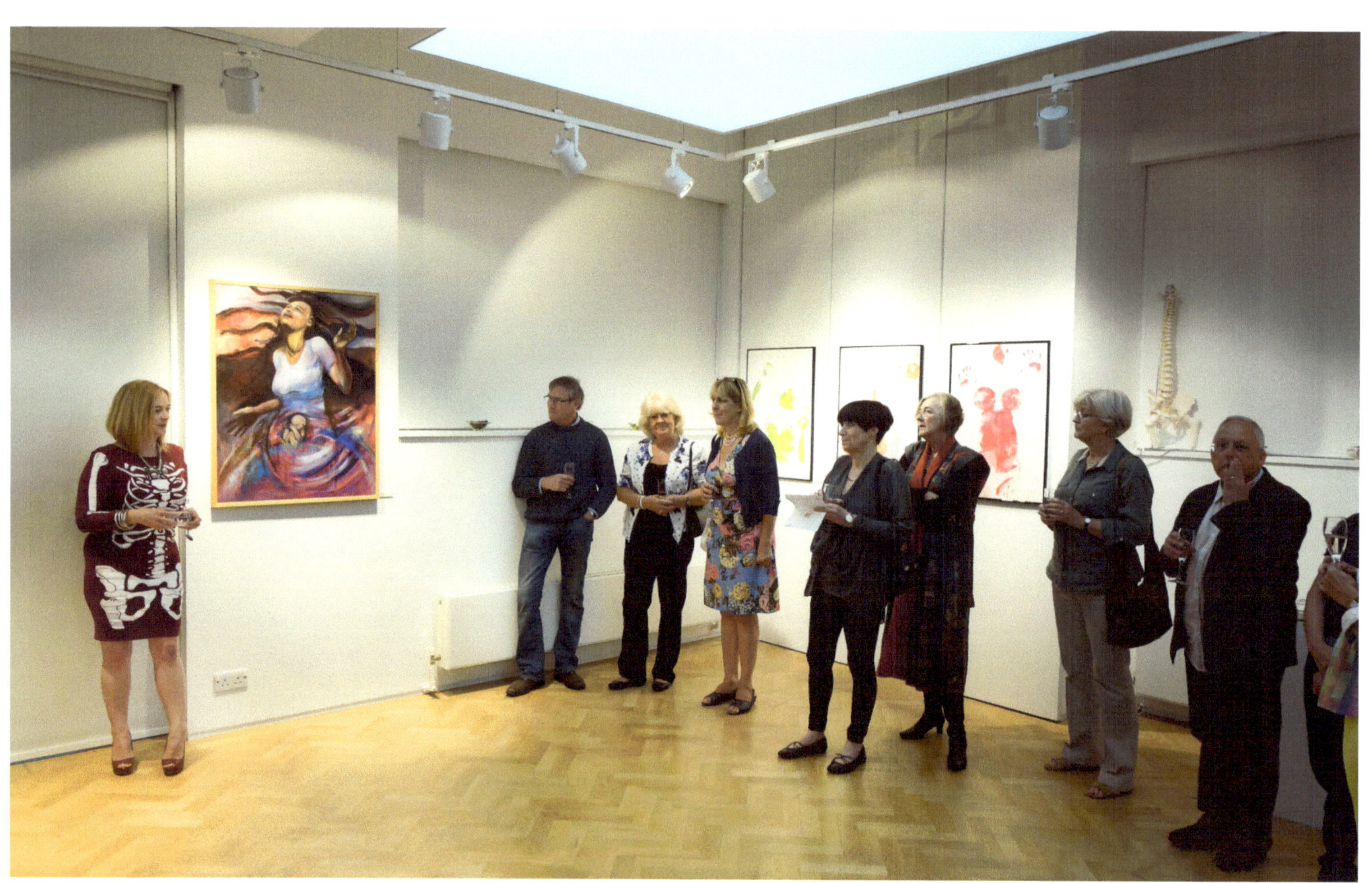

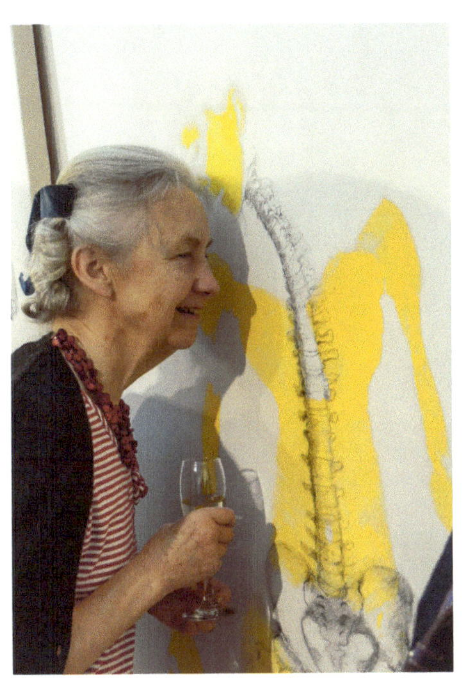

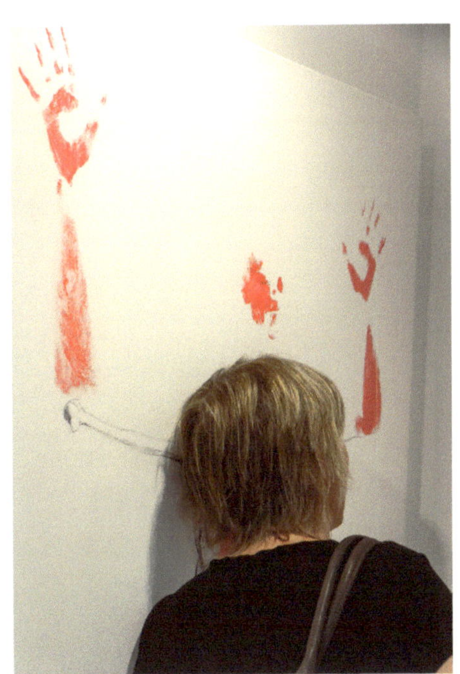

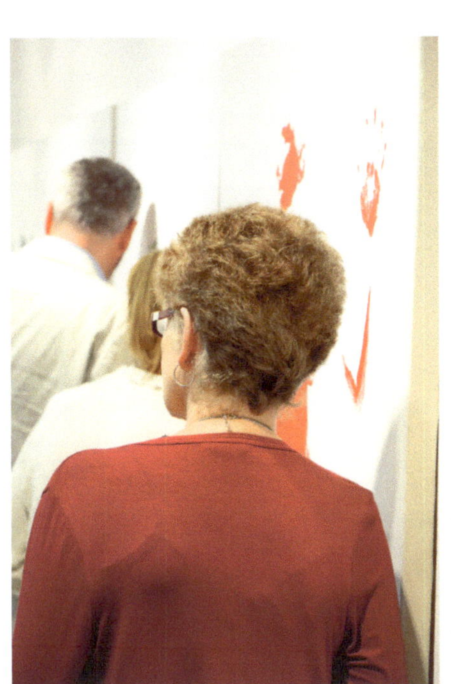

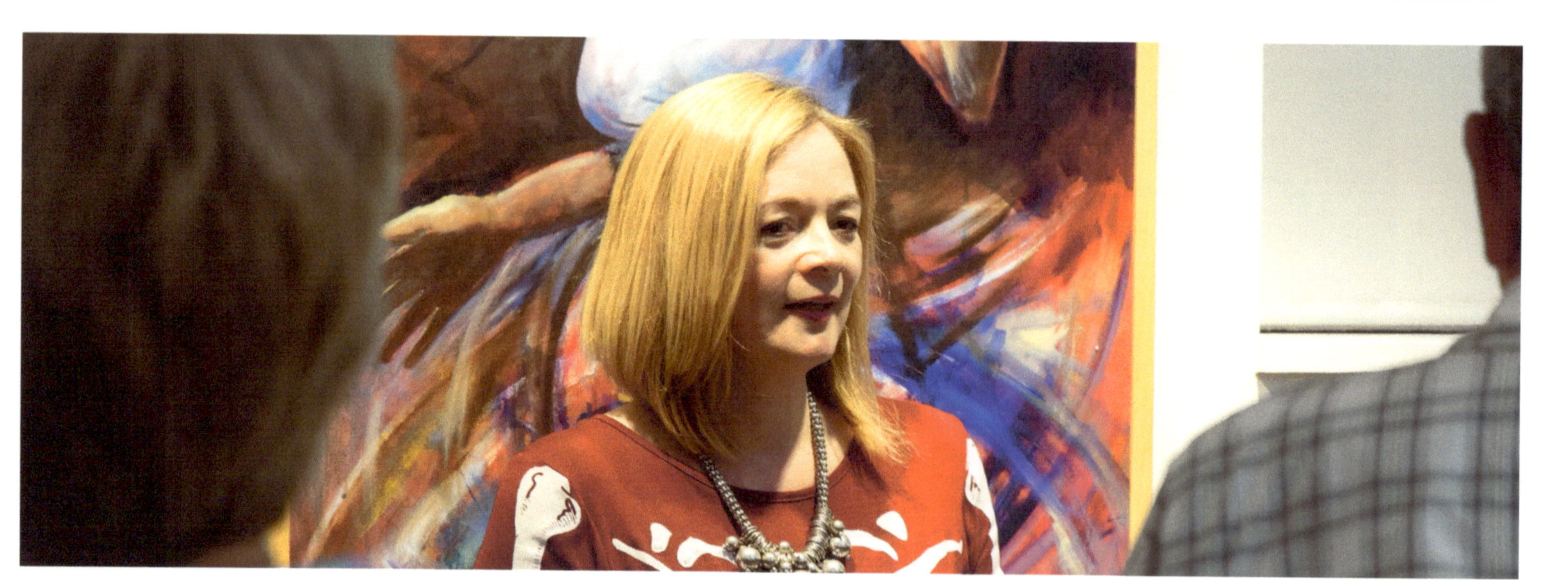

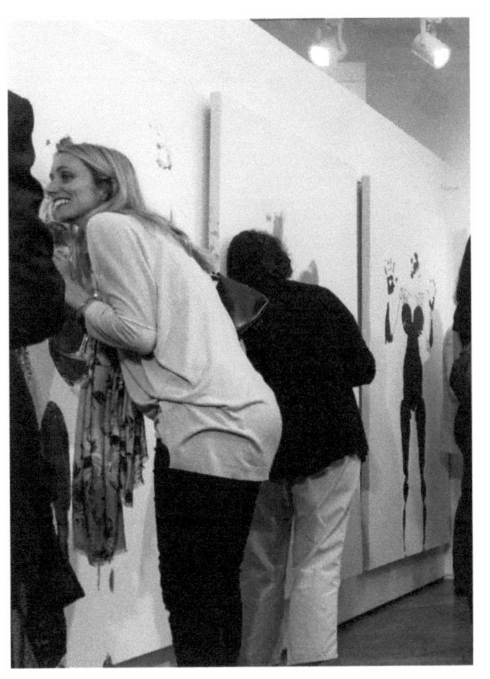

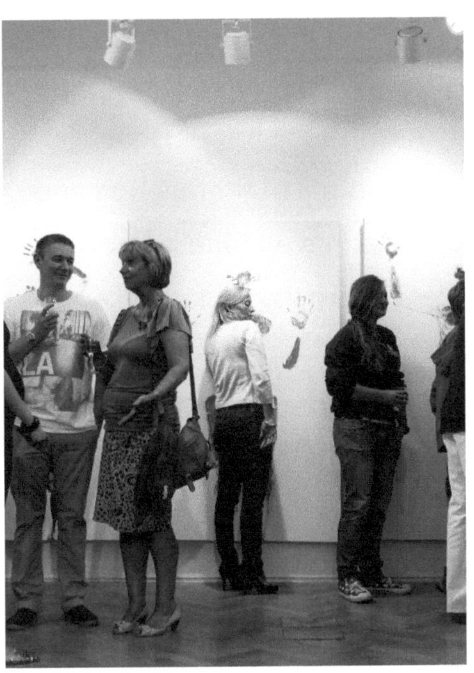

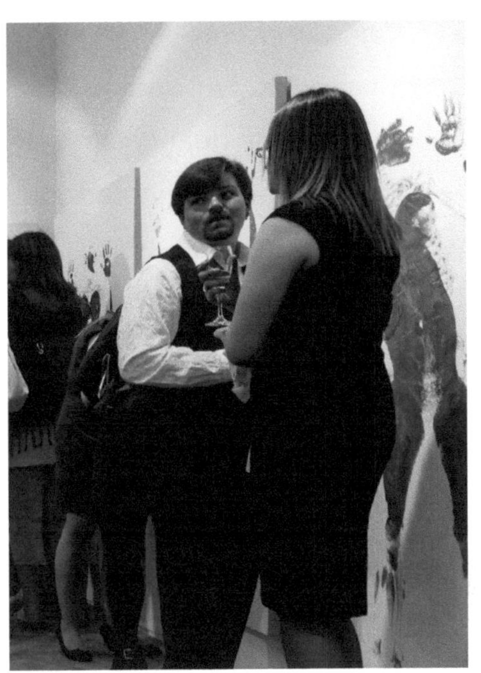

Exhibition Description

For some time now I have been developing a piece of work using Body-printing, sound and figure drawing to explore notions of beauty and self-worth in women. I have also audio-recorded women talking about their perceptions of themselves and what they think beauty is. The models that have done the body-print are models from all walks of life and many different ages, belief structures and different nationalities. It has been amazing to record sound as part of the installation as I had not anticipated the impact it would have on the models. So many of them left the studio, excited and inspired by the process of taking part in it. All of them spoke of it as a liberating experience.

The inspiration for the sound element came from a long standing fascination with using sound in art and more directly from visiting the Susan Hiller exhibition at the Tate in May 2011, specifically seeing the piece "Witness".

"Upper Room" is about beauty, faith and belief in one's self and perhaps God. The idea of presenting multiple images of women led me to look at various groupings of people in art. The piece by Chris Ofili "The Upper Room" has Fascinated me and it inspired the layout for the configuration which echoes that of Christ and the twelve disciples; in my piece the Christ figure is represented by a pregnant woman, the Madonna perhaps?

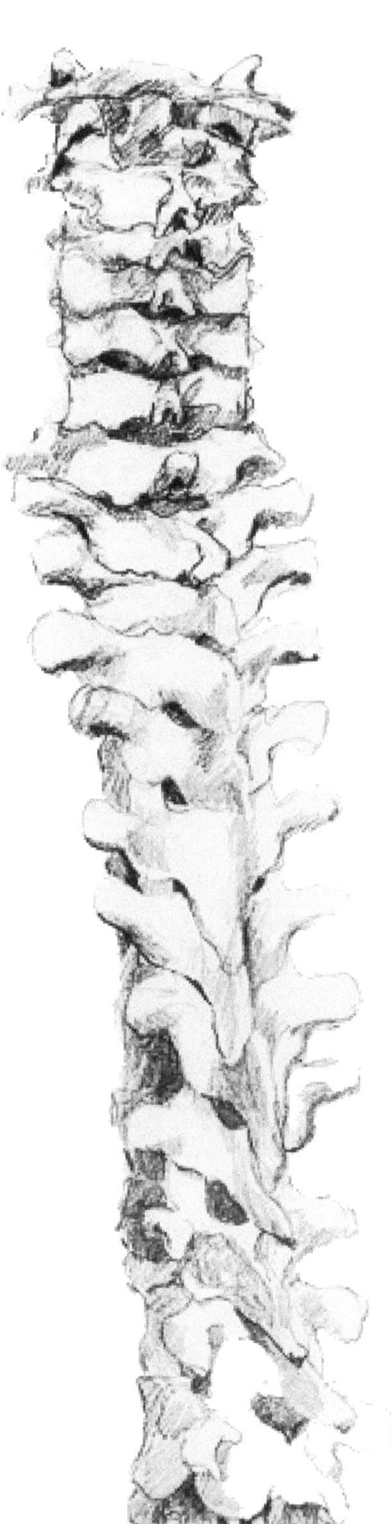

The installation is called "Upper Room" but it is not the male "Upper Room" which we can read about in the Bible. Instead, it presents and celebrates women who are so often the witnesses to key moments in history and yet are so often air-brushed from history. The piece presents the very real and visceral presence of these women.

The sound, such an important part of the piece, takes it from being just a room of images to being a space with a presence; a room full of women talking/ whispering their story. A story of how they view themselves and how they think others view them.

As the viewer stands in the space they are drawn in to the room at first by what they see, but then by the chance to catch a piece of dialogue almost as one overhearing a private conversation......

Deborah Last
www.deborahlast.co.uk

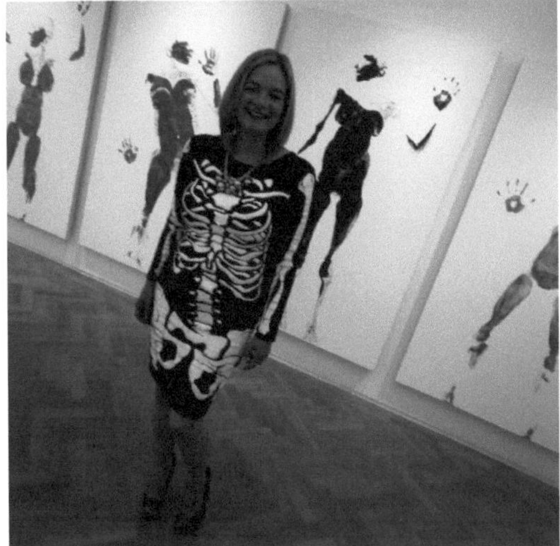

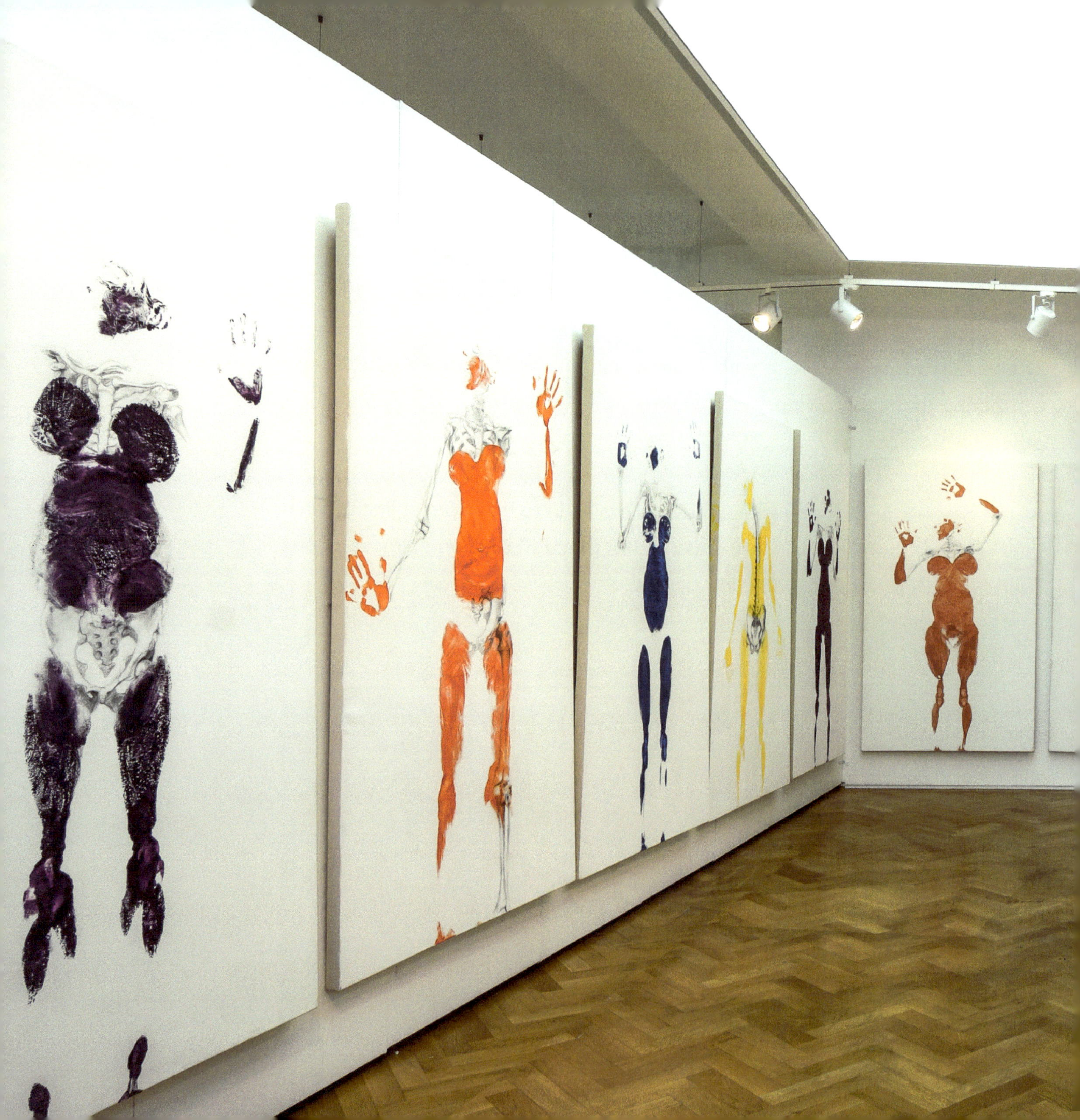

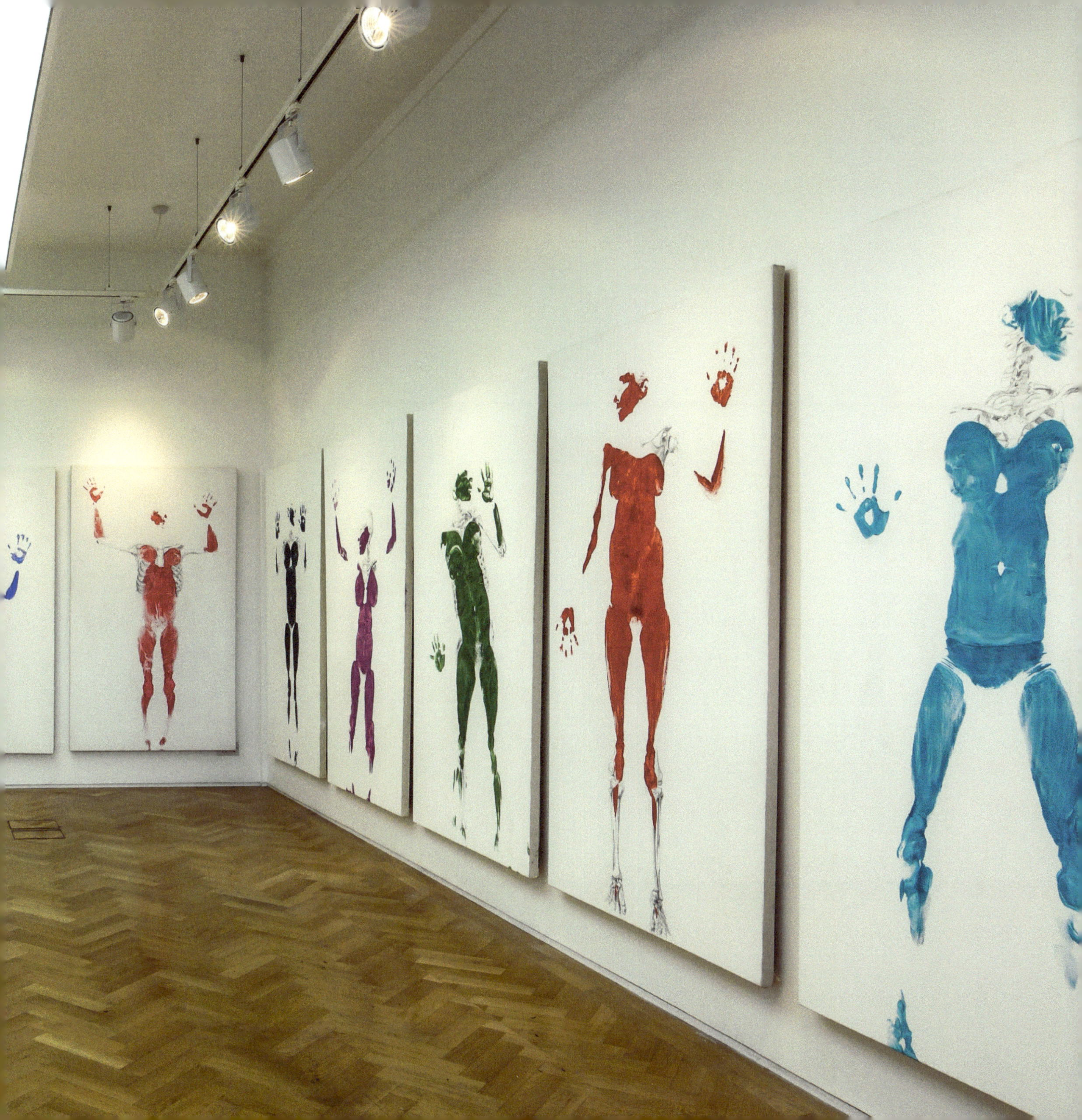

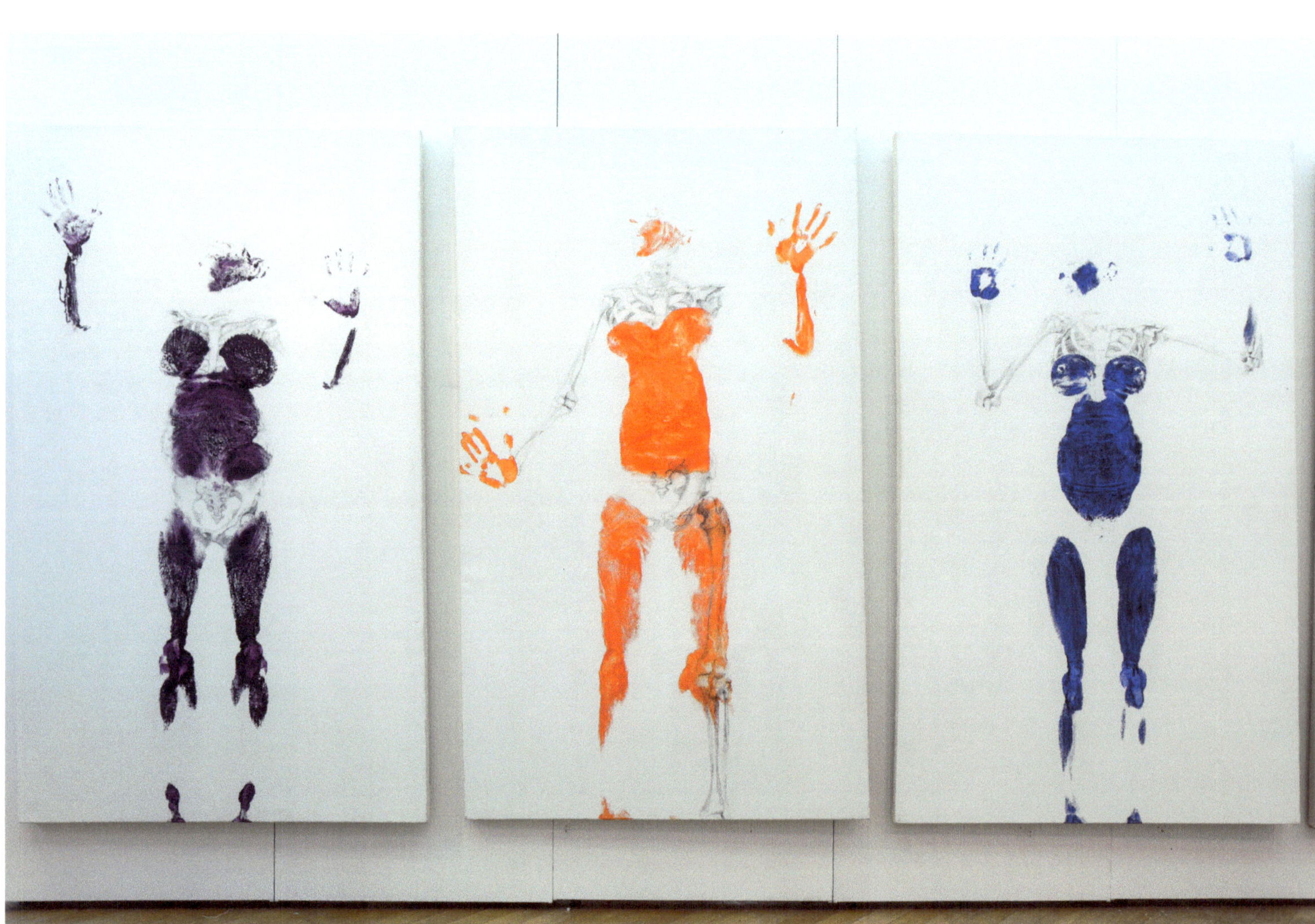

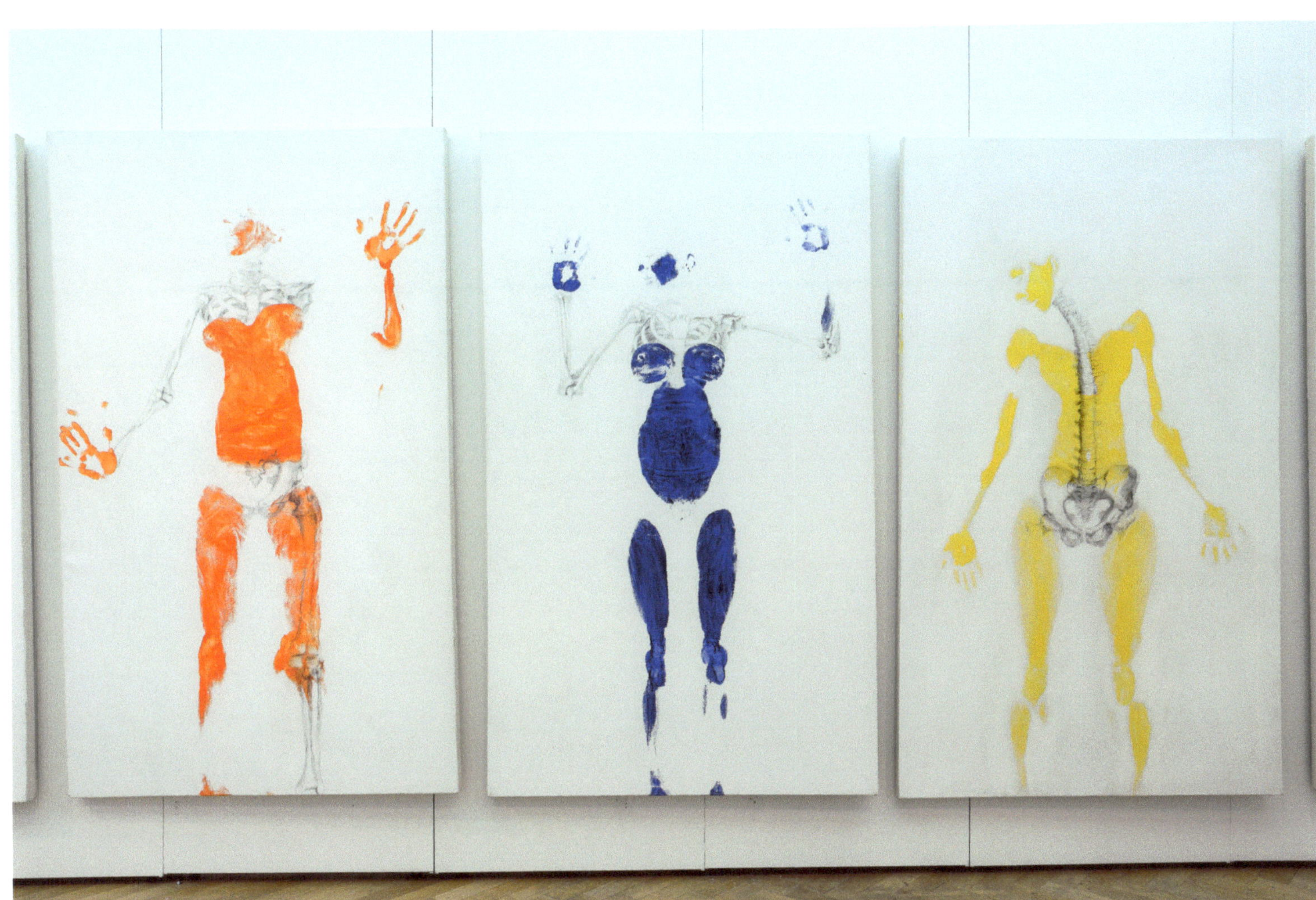

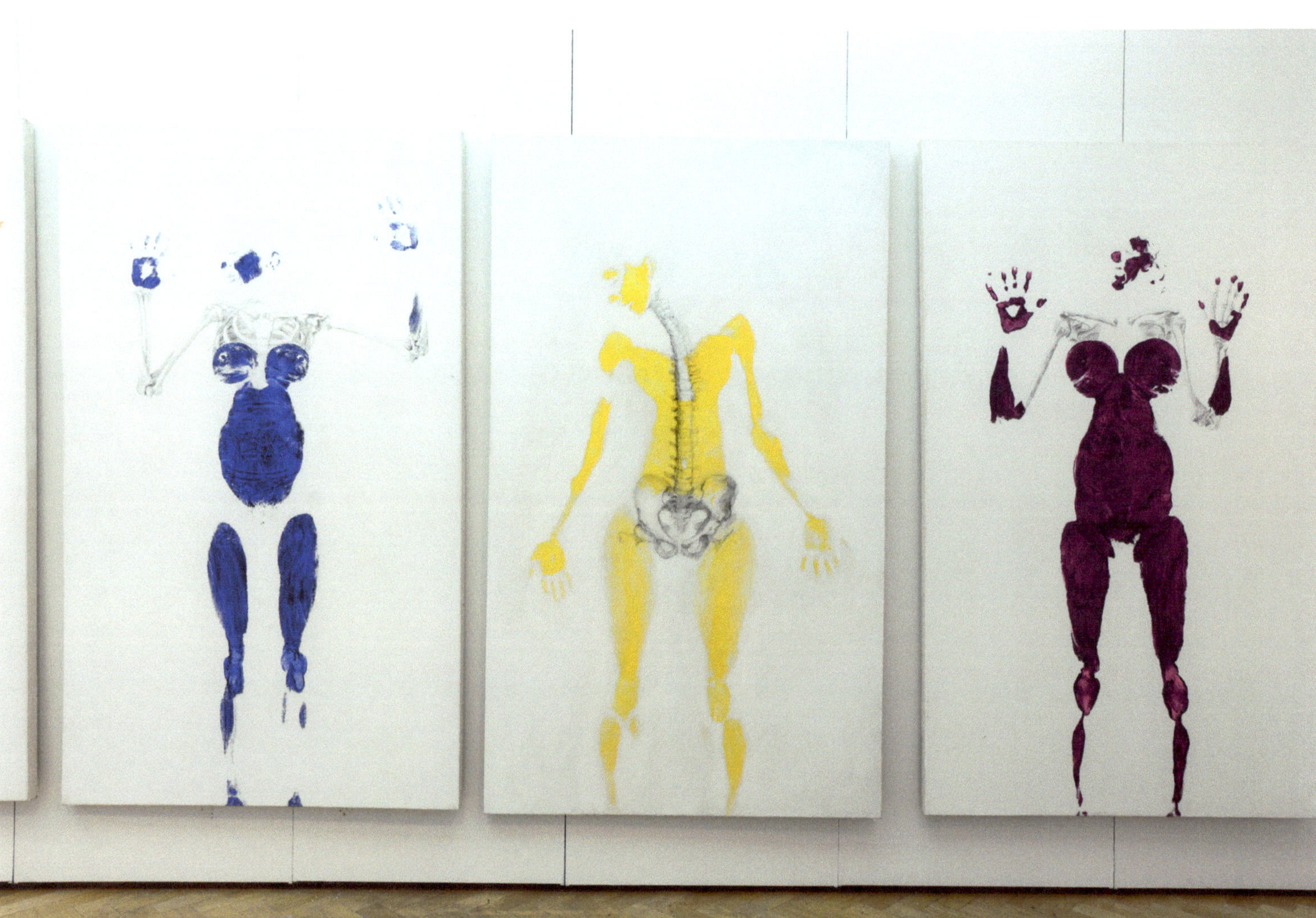

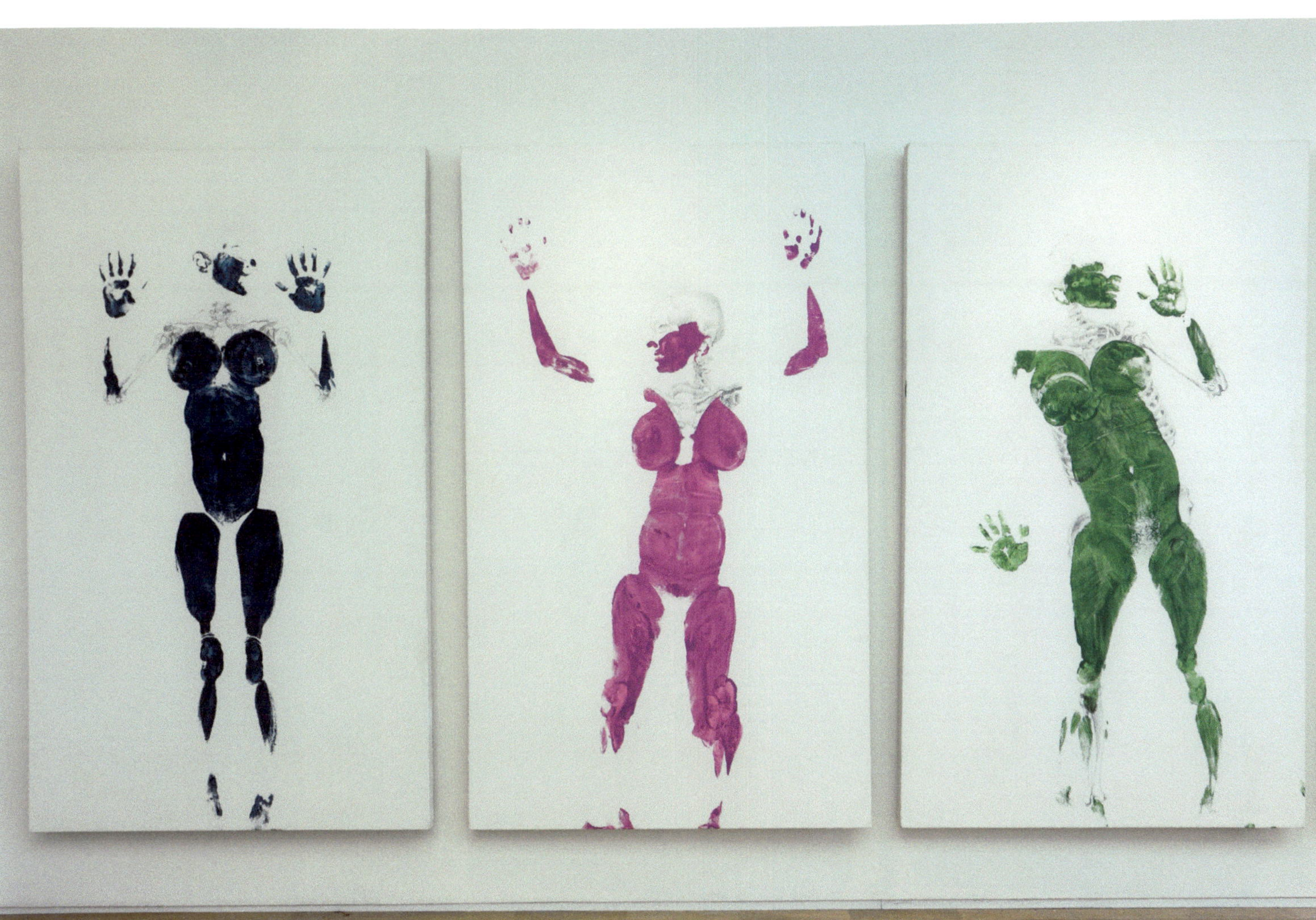

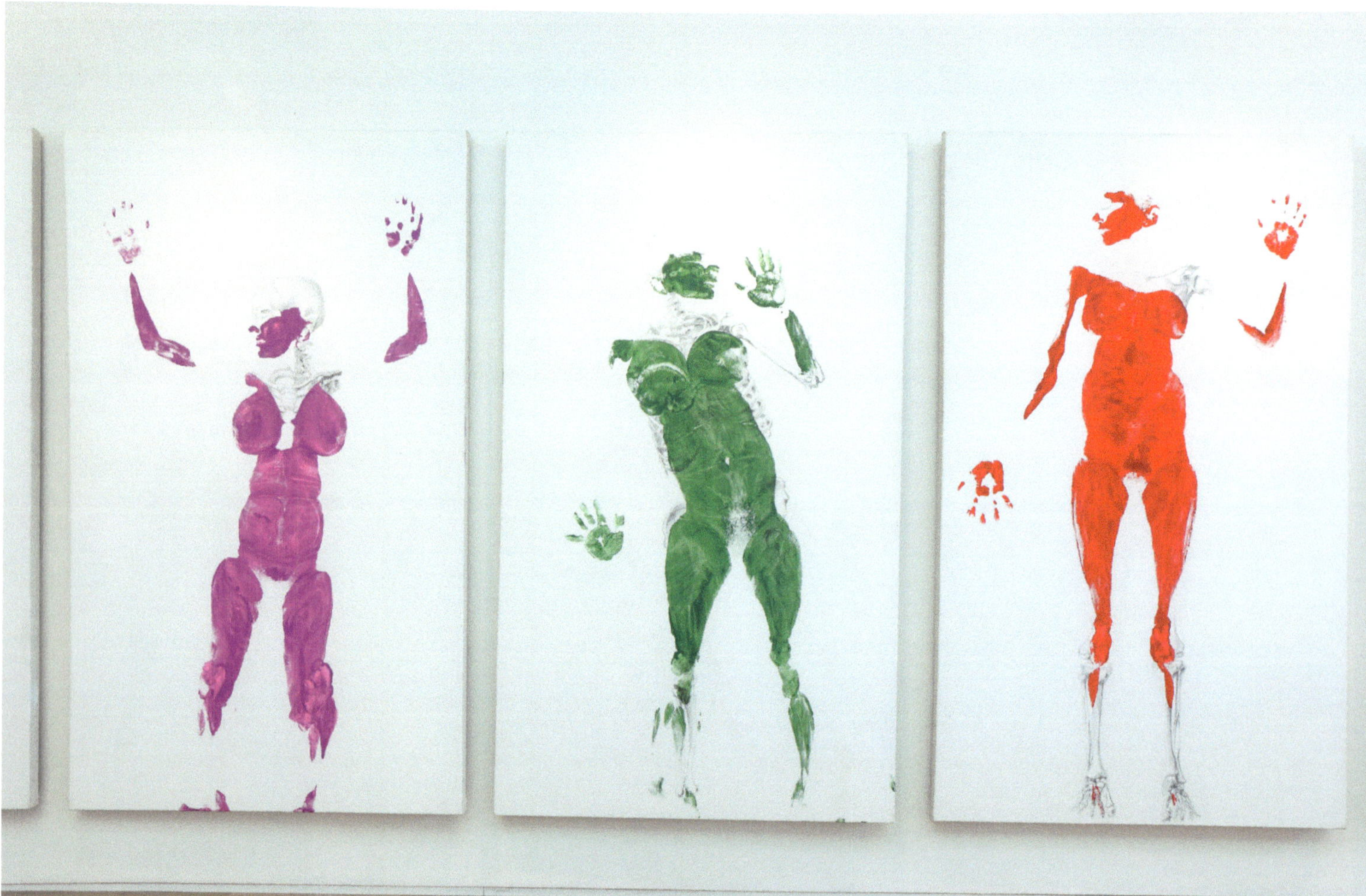

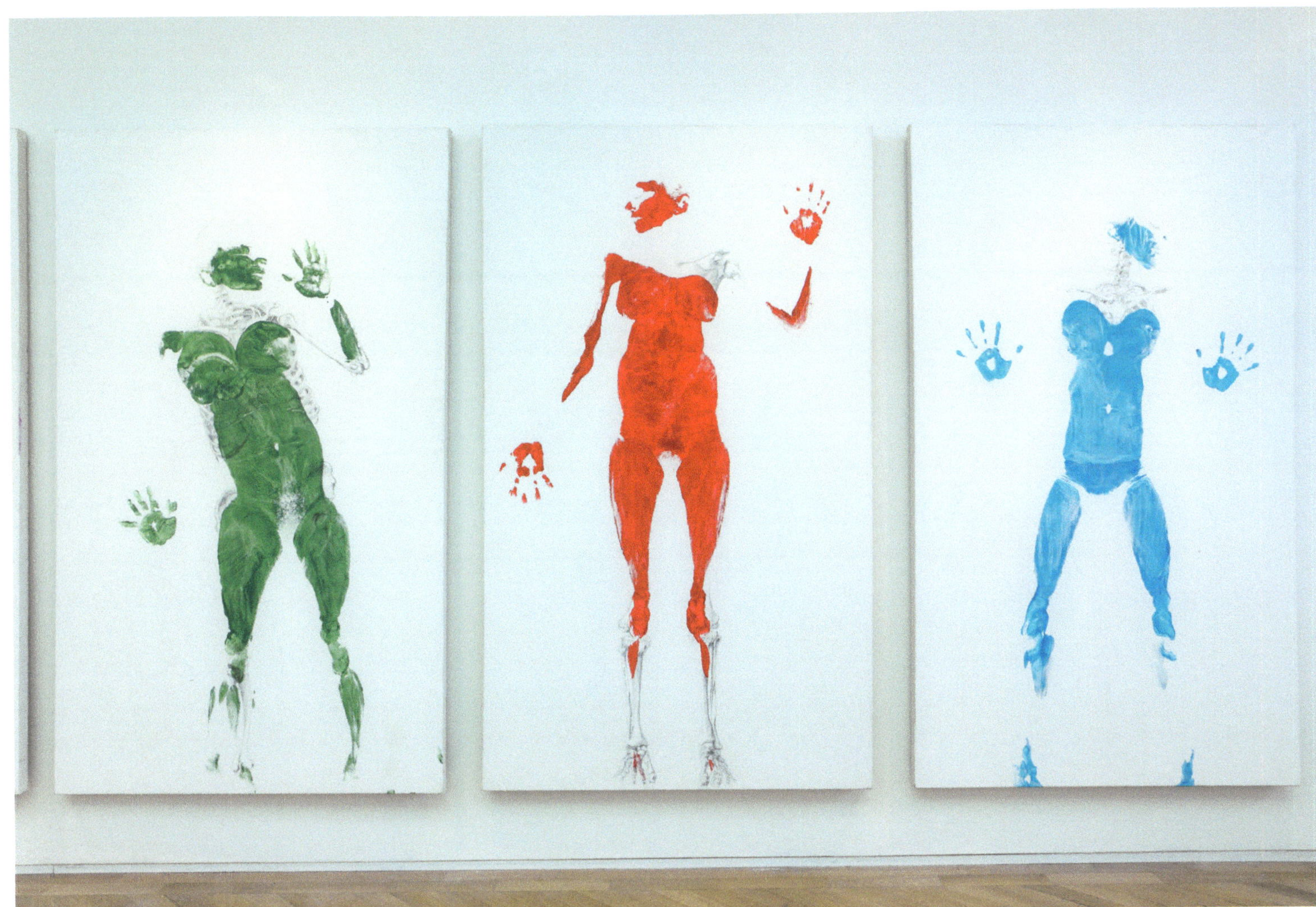

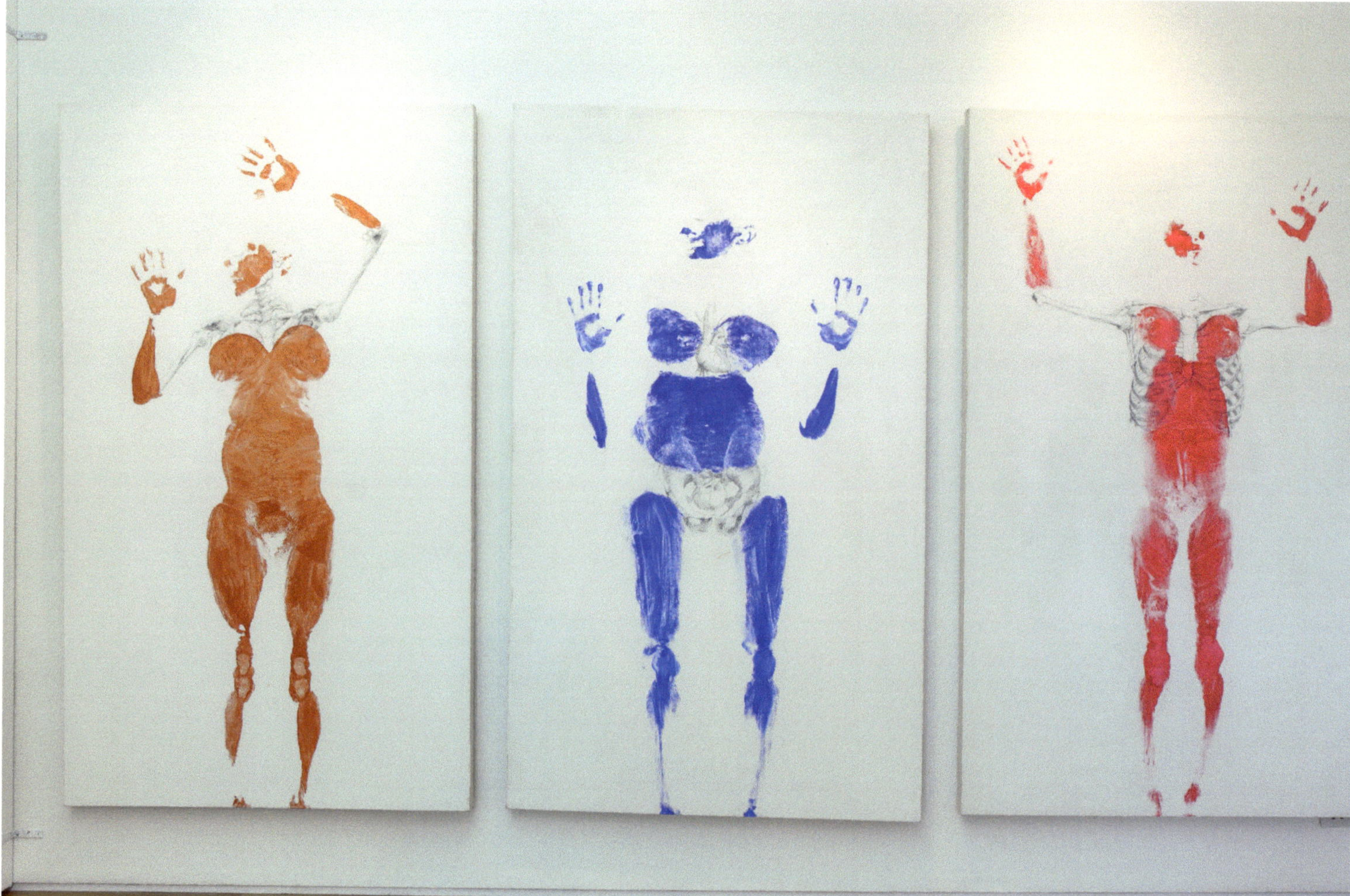

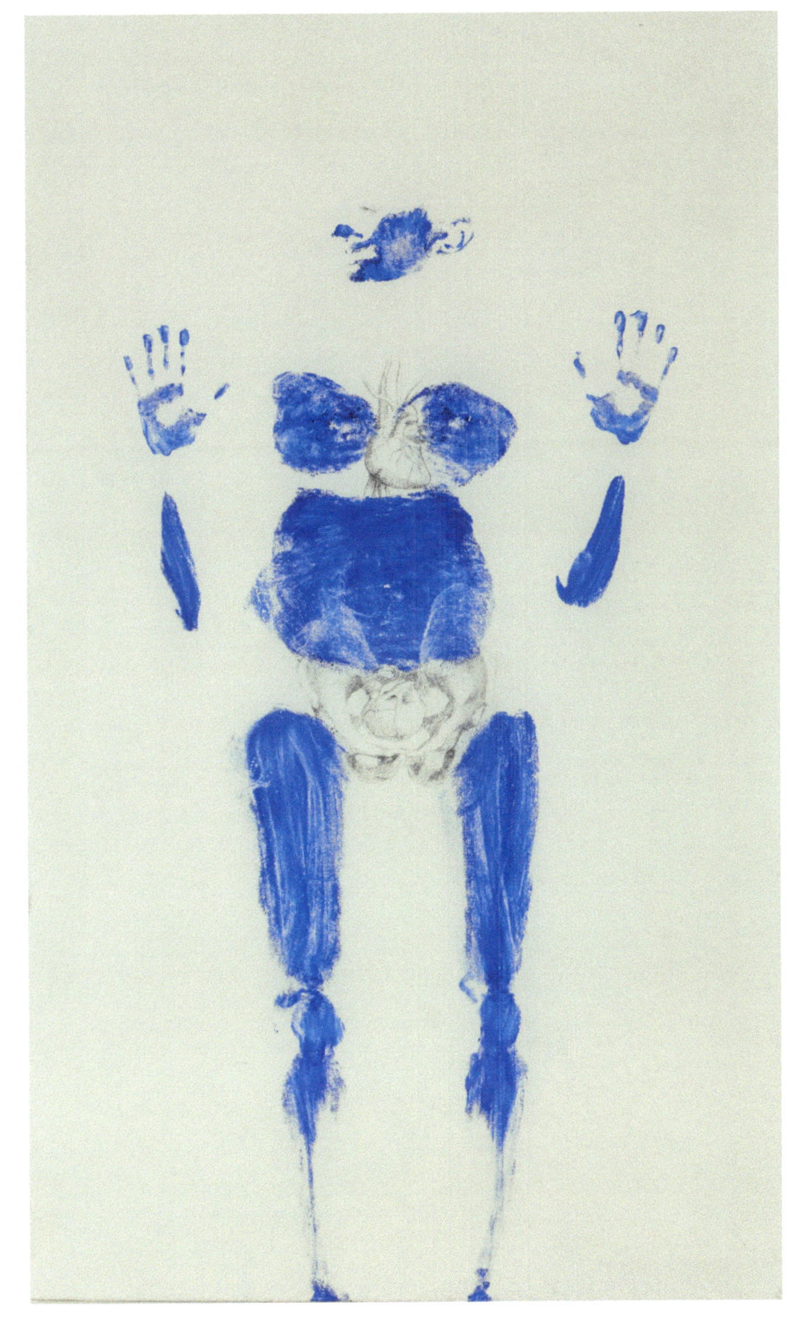

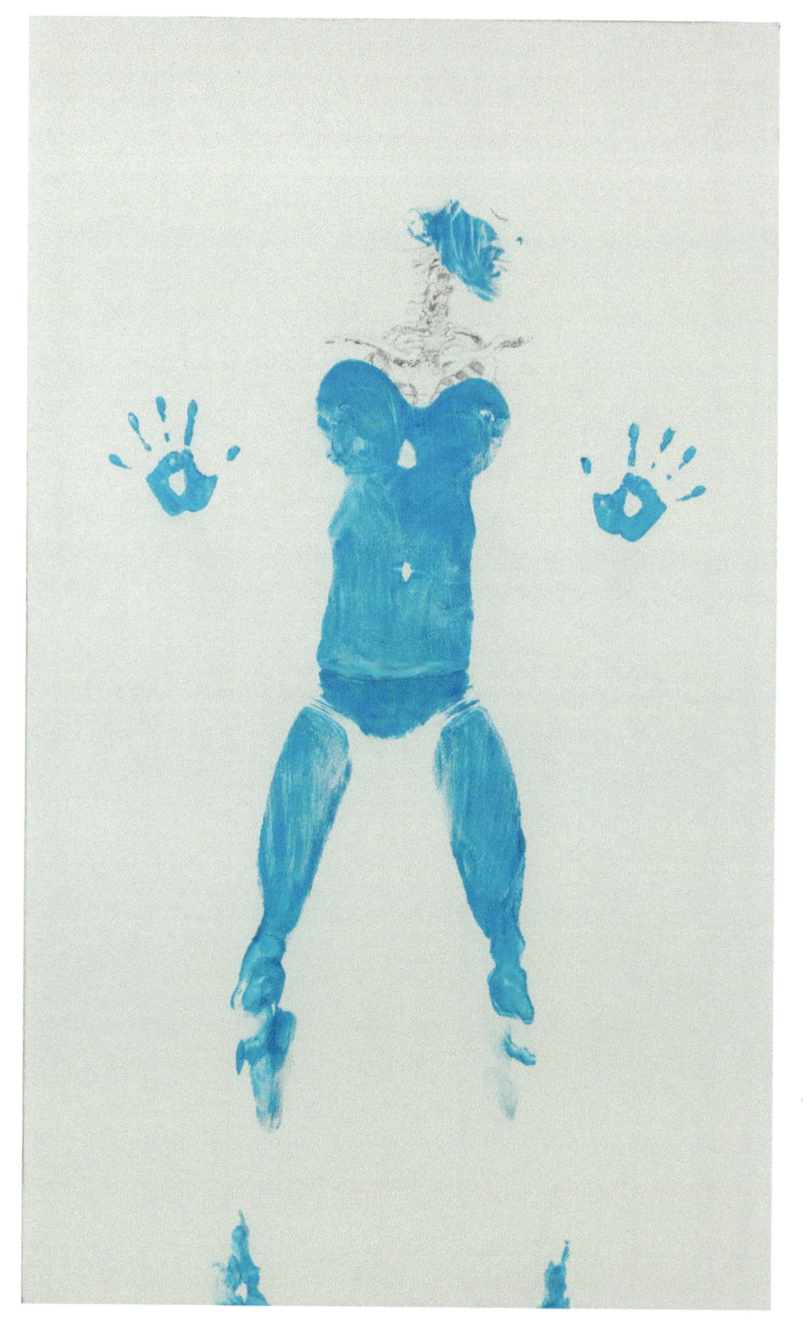

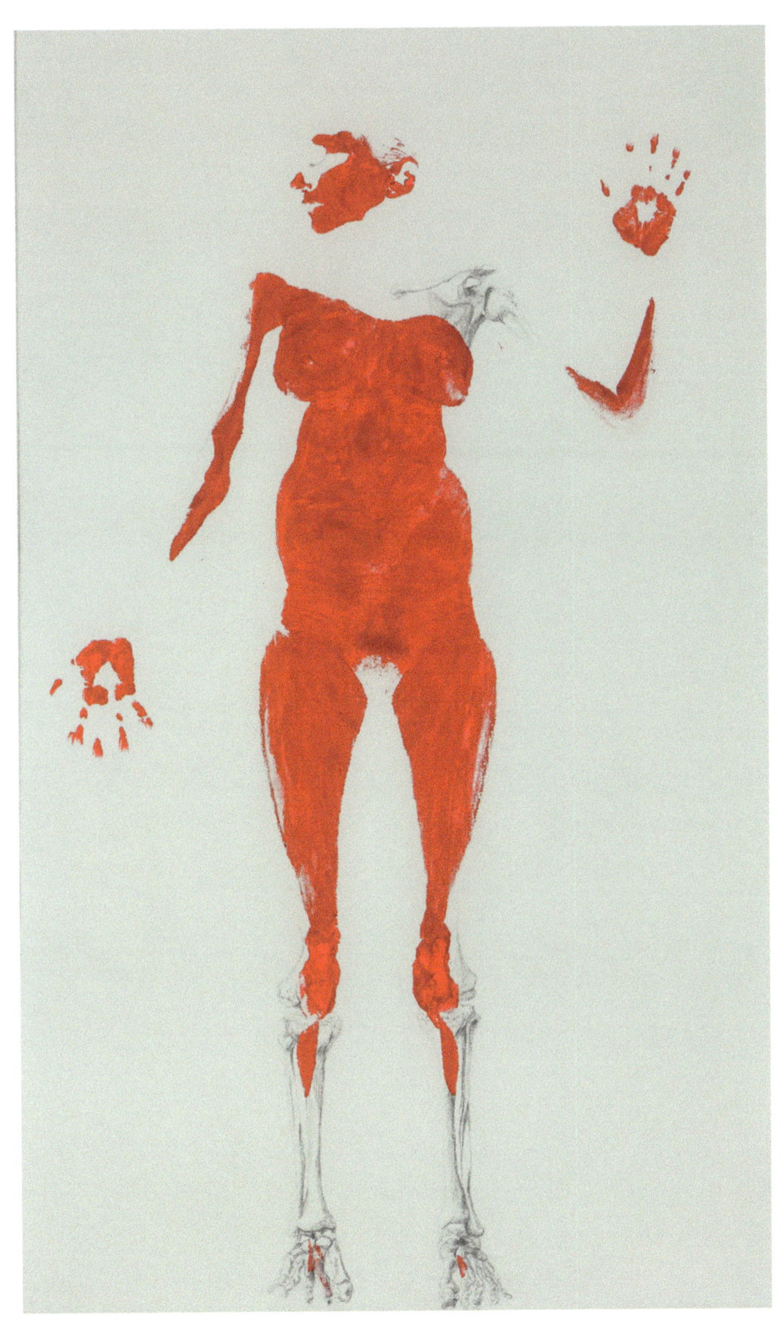

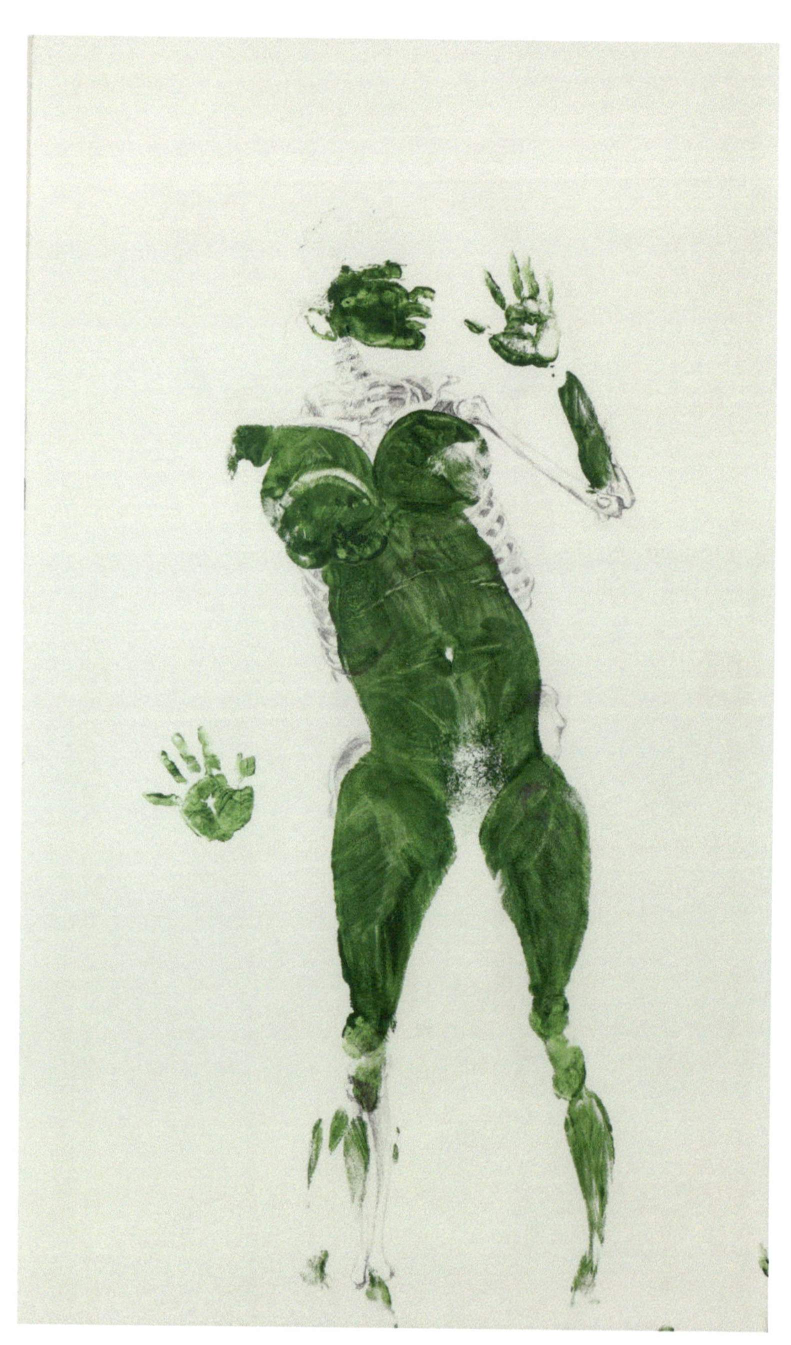

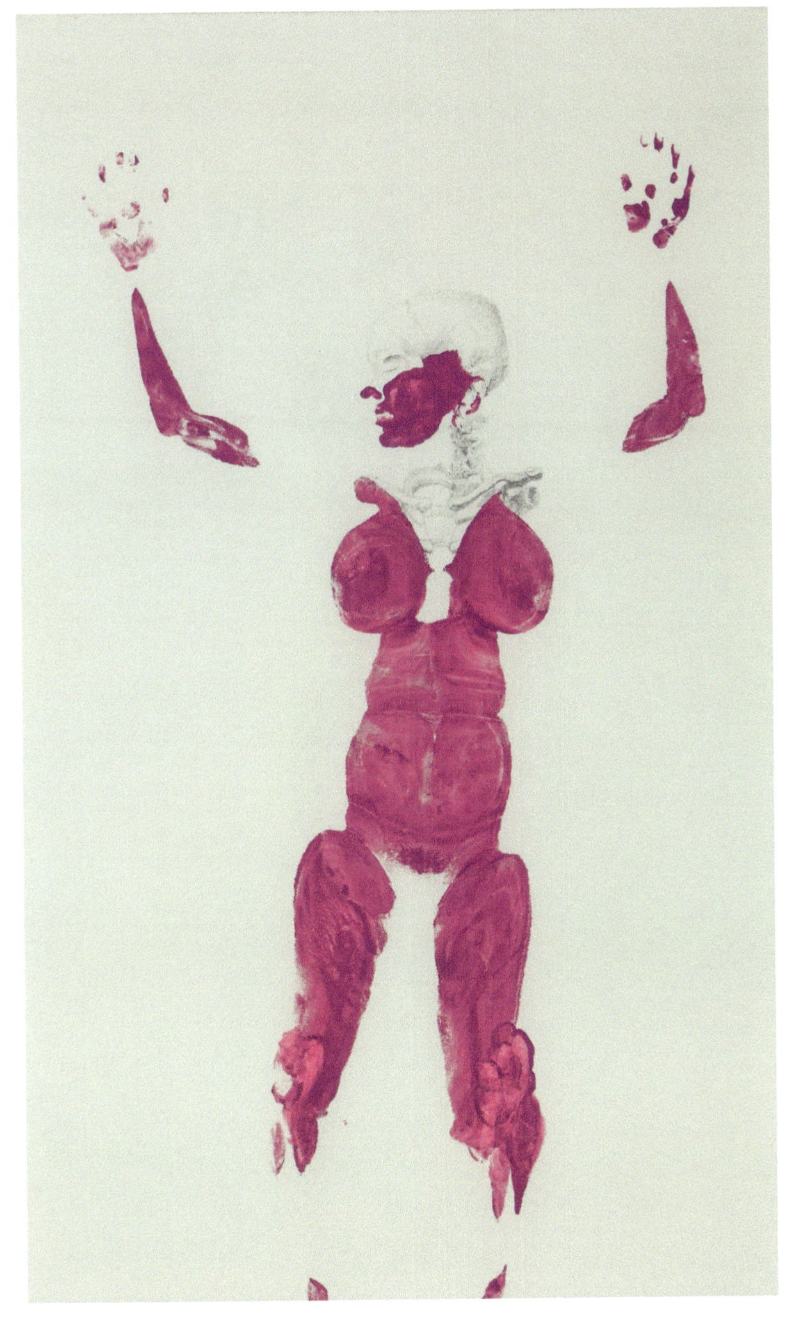

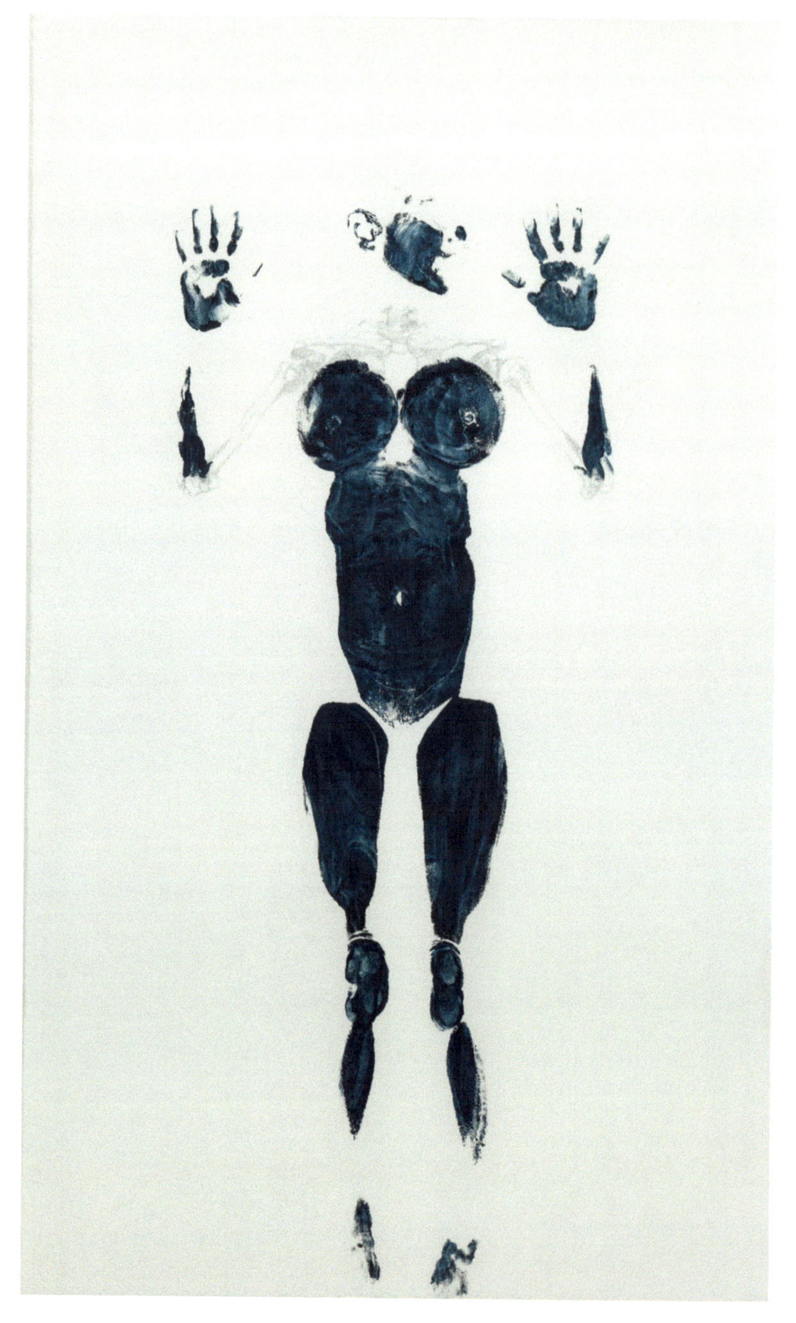

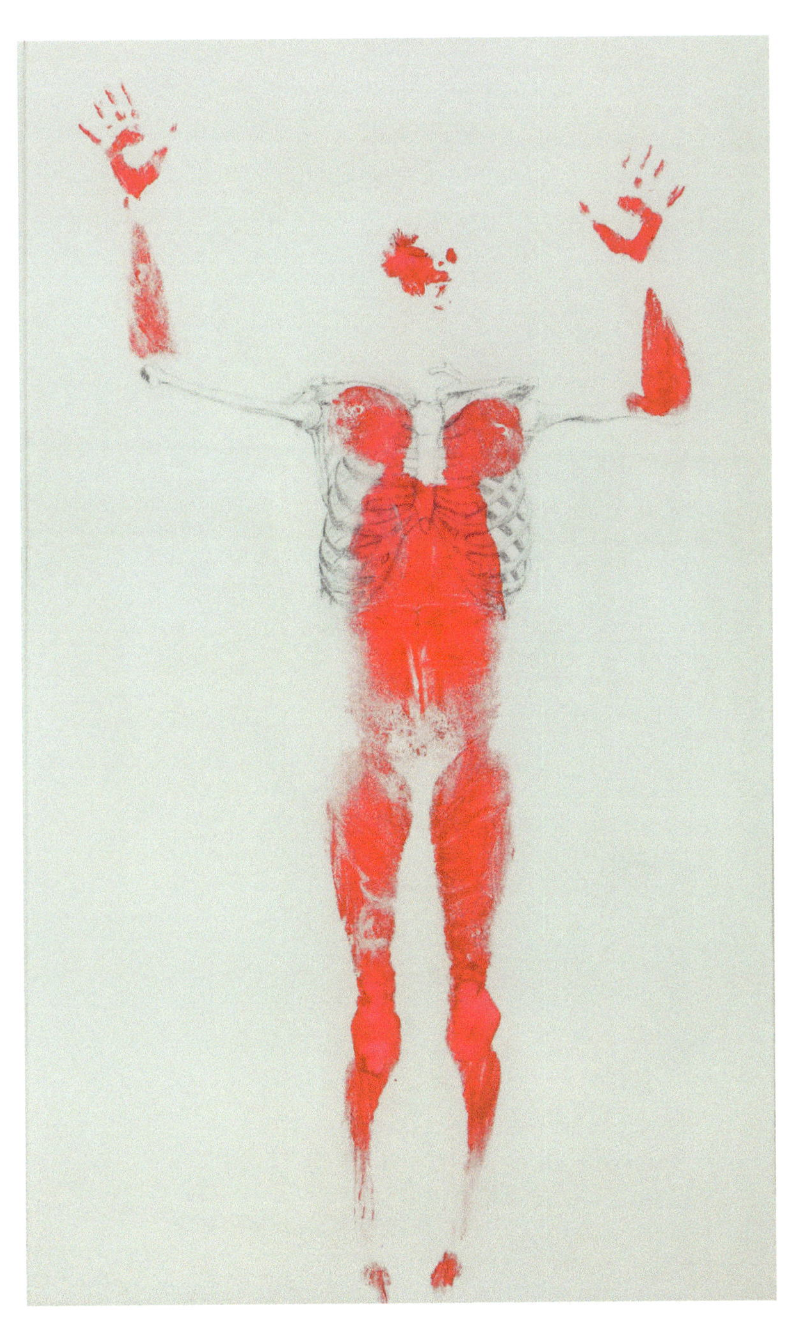

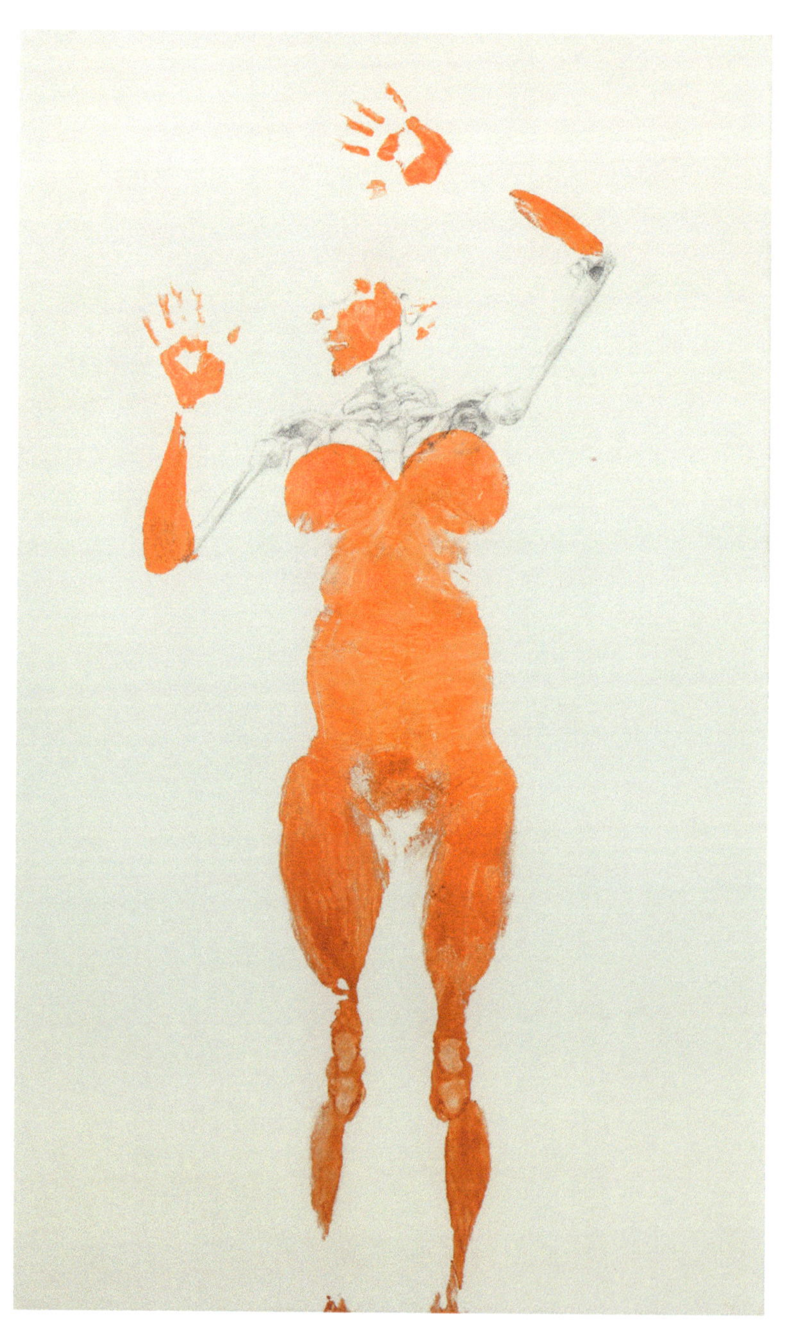

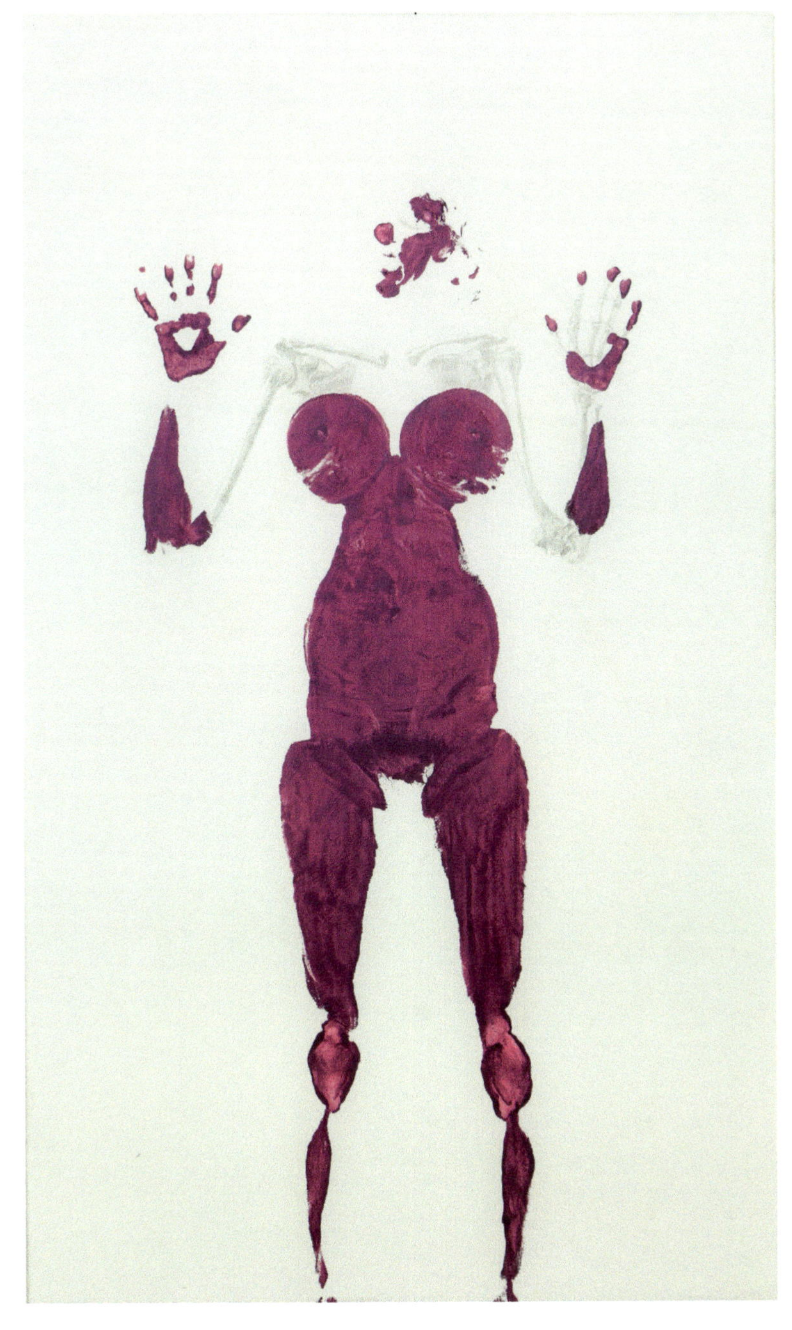

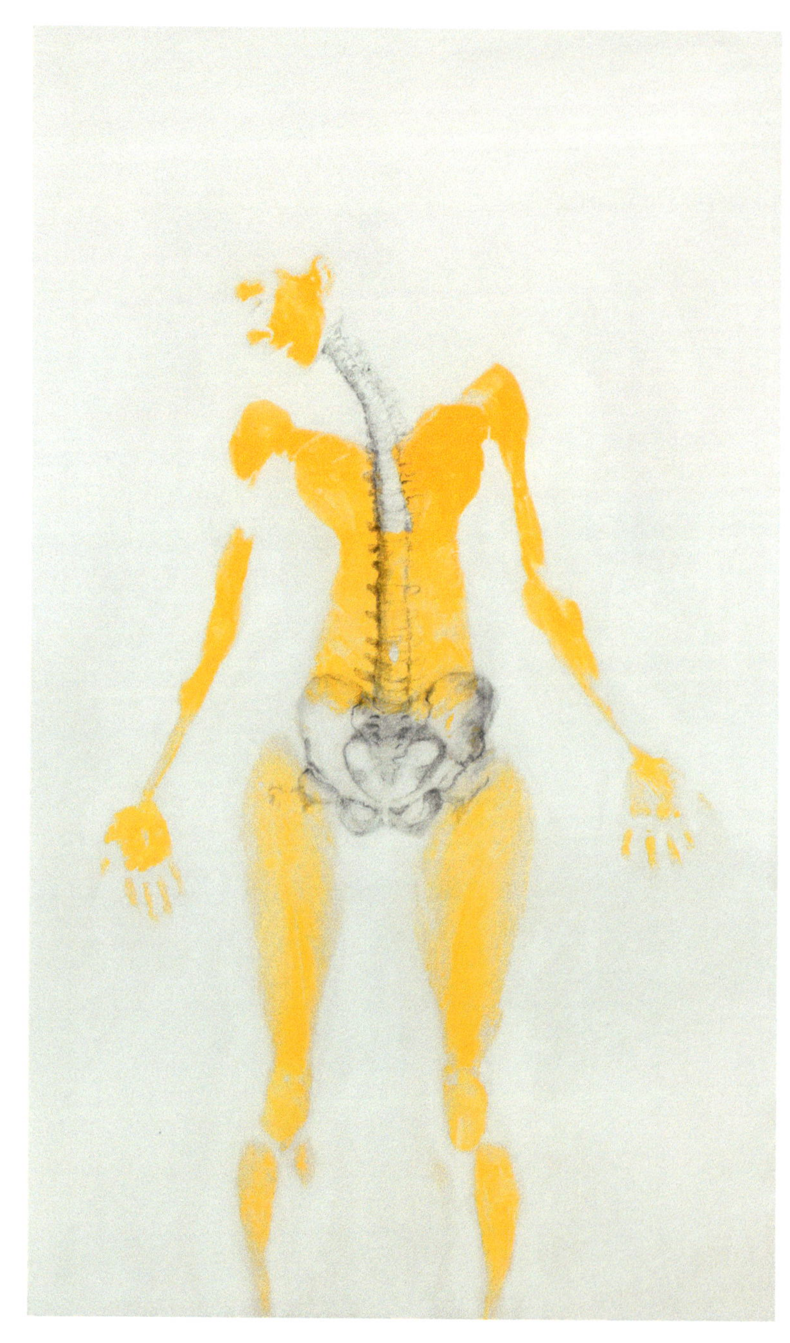

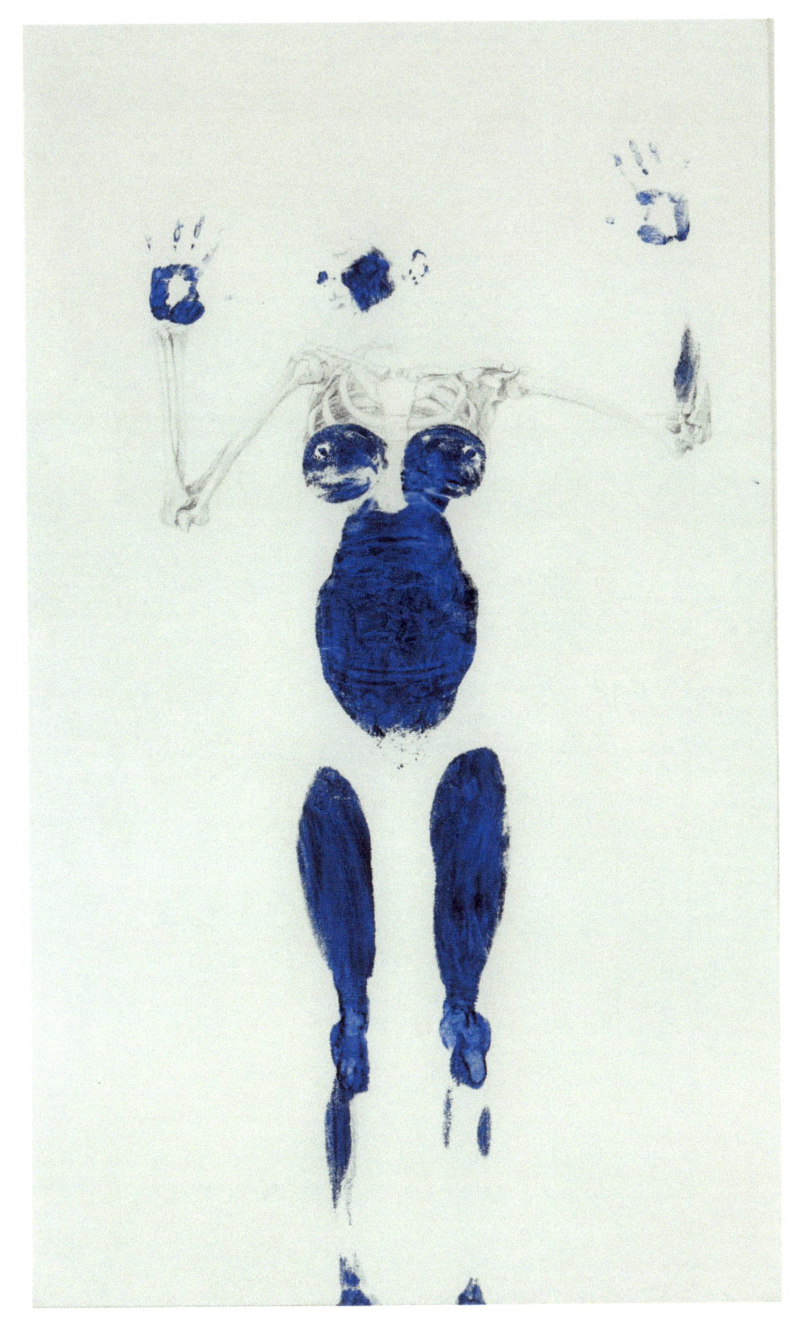

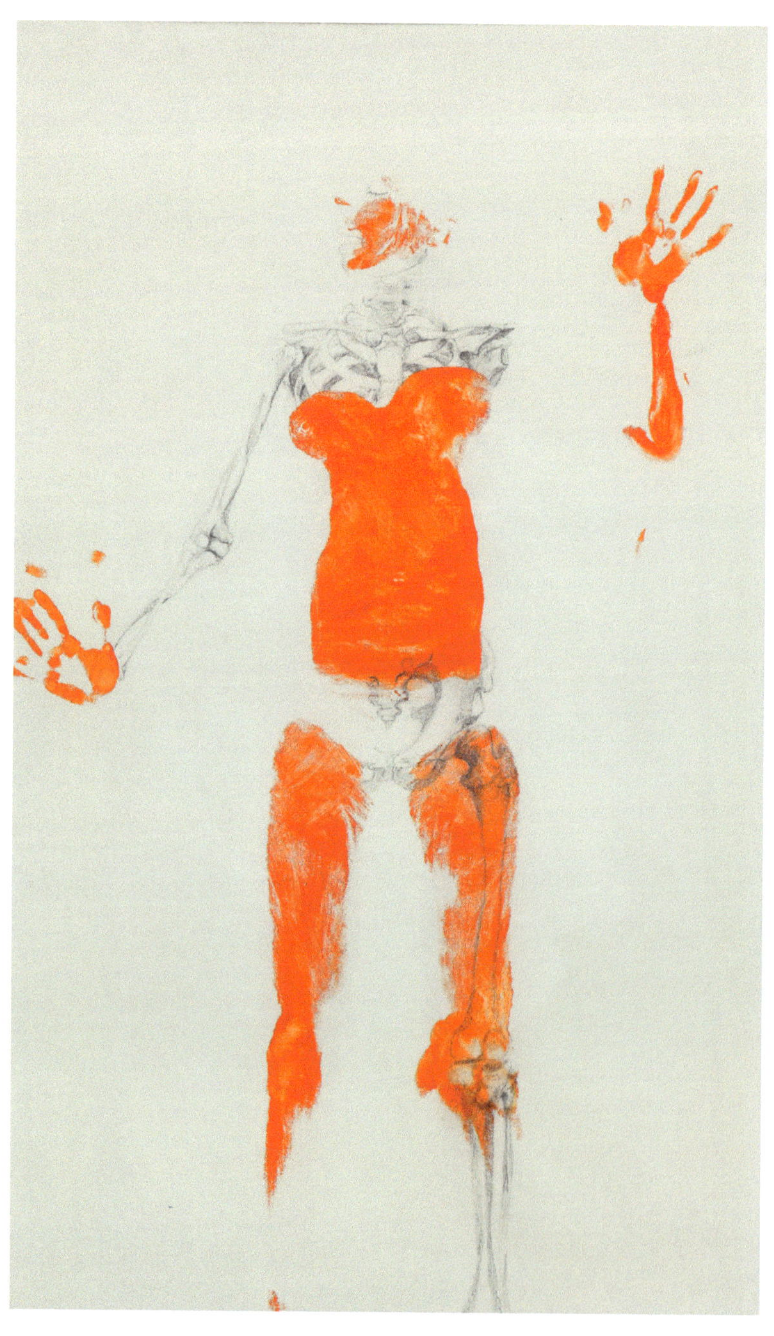

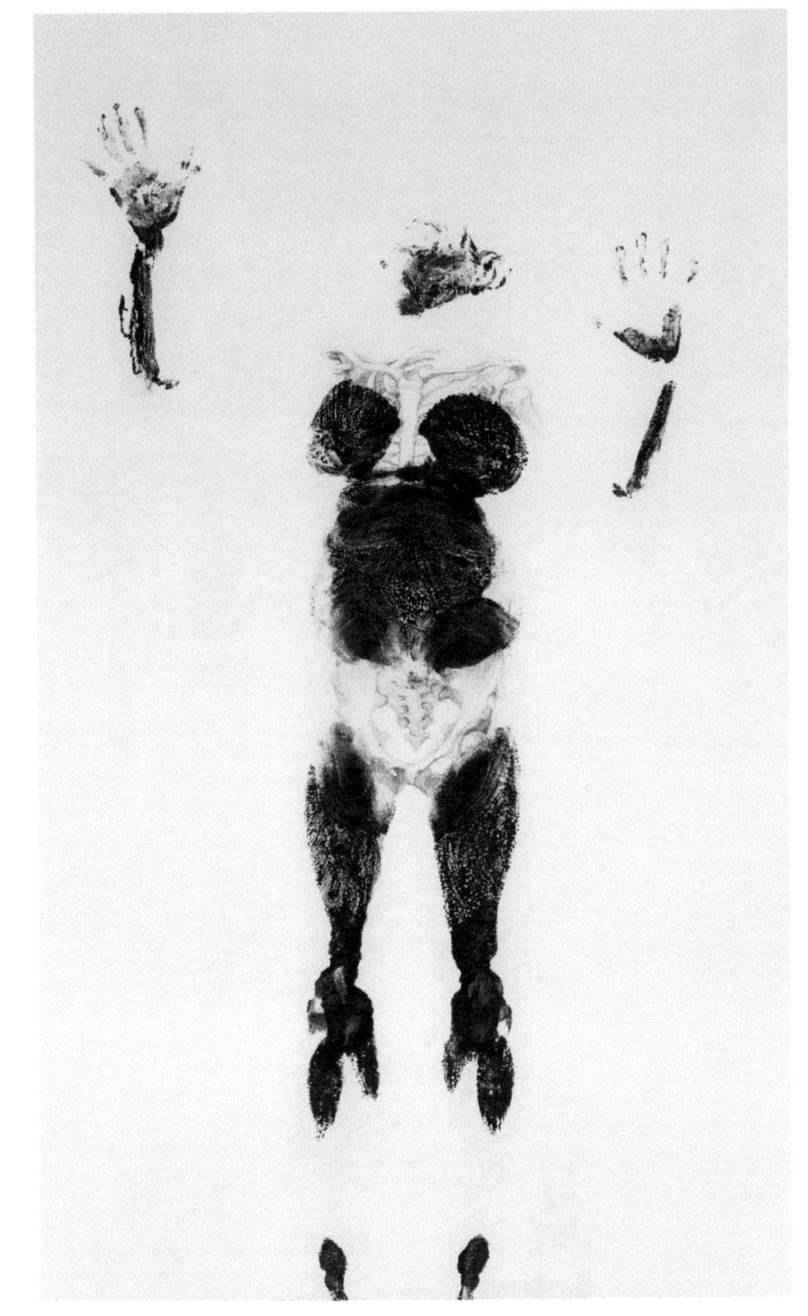

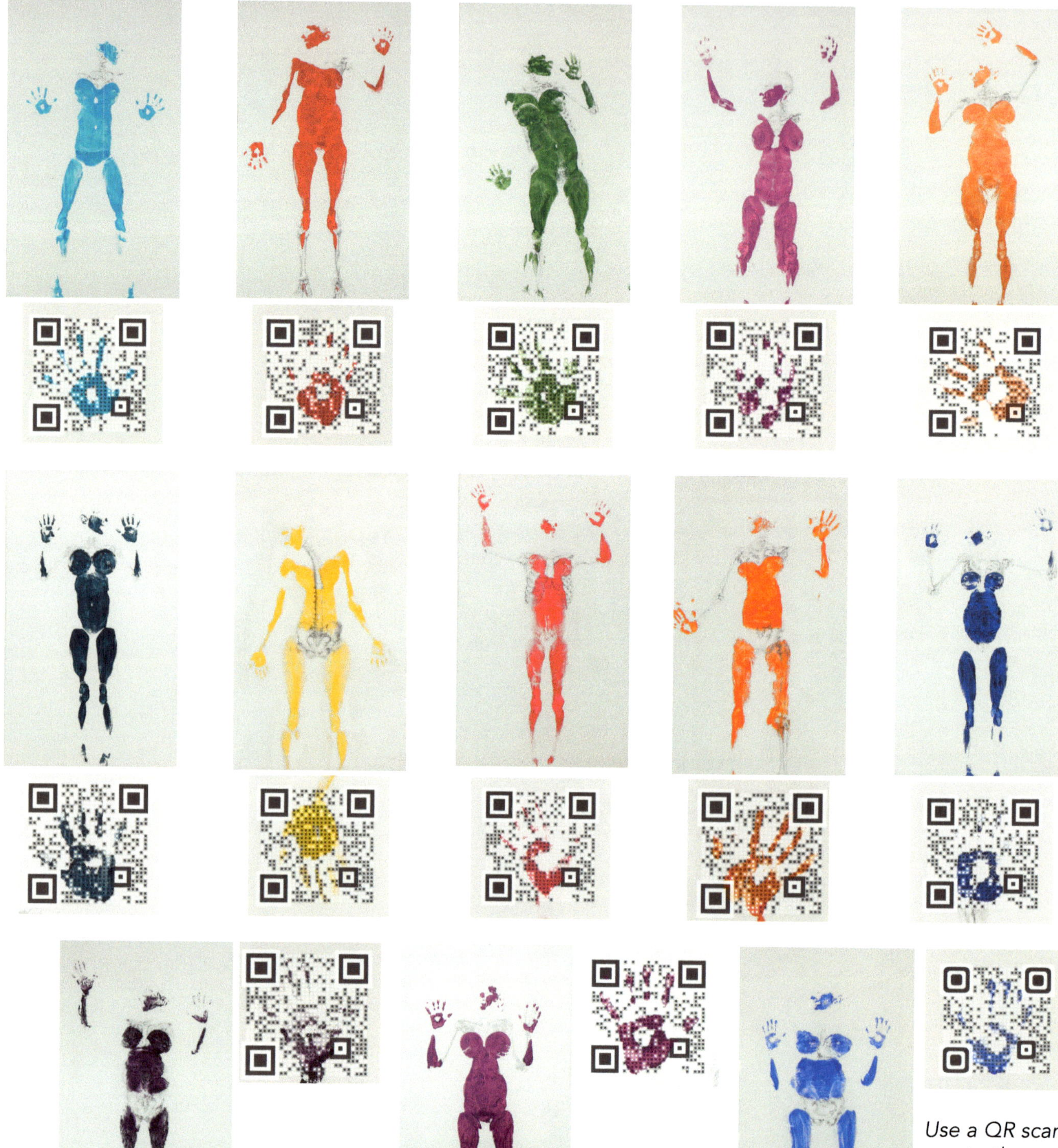

Use a QR scanner to take you to the web pages with the sound of each of the canvases

Deborah Last: Artist

www.deborahlast.co.uk

Deborah Last is a professional artist working from her studio within the beautiful Stowe Landscape gardens. She works directly from life and from memory to create light filled work within a narrative context.

Having spent 7 years living in India working as an artist and tutor, her work retains the love of colour and story that so inspired her whilst she was there.

Deborah has an honours degree in Ceramics & Glass and a Post Graduate certificate in Art education. In order to further her exceptional life drawing skills, she recently spent time studying anatomy with Dr Sarah Simblet and Professor Brian Crook at the Ruskin, Oxford University.

Her work is held in private collections throughout the UK, including Sir Richard FitzHerbert of Tissington Hall, Derbyshire, and Sir Jack Hayward.

She owns Buckingham Art School with her fellow artist and friend Zoë Day
She is a Patron and a founding member of Buckingham Art for All.

For sales, commissions or to book a talk, demo or workshop please contact:

dlast@btinternet.com

People to thank...

Family who have been amazingly supportive as I have used lots of time and a fair bit of money to put this together.

A huge thank you to all the women who have done the body prints and those who have been happy to have their insightful thoughts and memories recorded.

Daniel Hobden the sound designer, Luke Hemming for helping him put it all together, Ollie Goddard for the book design, Roger Goddard for the official photos and the ones he took at the private view, Andy Winter for photos of the private view, Zoë Day for her creative input, Seonad McHugh for help with the words and helping work out how to say what I wanted to say! Professor Lynne Cameron for proof reading and content checks. To the "Five Women Artist Group"; for your ongoing encouragement.

Amanda Jorgensen and Deborah Clarke for having the exhibition in the gallery at Stowe School and enabling the wonderful photographs and a very well received first view for Upper Room.

www.ingramcontent.com/pod-product-compliance
Ingram Content Group UK Ltd.
Pitfield, Milton Keynes, MK11 3LW, UK
UKHW060101300726
14090UKWH00003B/339

* 9 7 8 0 9 9 2 8 8 4 2 9 1 *